P9-DVJ-668

Bernadette of Lourdes

"The simpler one writes, the better it will be.
In trying to dress things up, one only distorts them."

Saint Bernadette on her deathbed   April, 1879

Bernadette of Lourdes

A Life Based on
Authenticated Documents

by René Laurentin
Translated by John Drury

Winston Press   430 Oak Grove Minneapolis, MN 55403

Originally published in France
Vie de Bernadette
Copyright © 1978 Desclee de Brouwer

Copyright © 1979 by Winston Press, Inc.
Library of Congress Catalog Card Number: 79-62880
ISBN: 0-03-051156-9

All rights reserved. No part of this book may be
reproduced or used in any form without
written permission from Winston Press, Inc.
Printed in the United States of America.

Winston Press
430 Oak Grove
Minneapolis, MN 55403

5   4   3   2   1

Contents

WITHDRAWN

791147

Preface

One hundred years ago on April 16, 1879, Sister Marie Bernard Soubirous died in the convent of Saint Gildard in Nevers, France. Now, on the occasion of this anniversary, we have a new book covering her very brief life of thirty-five years.

For this book we are indebted to one of today's most knowledgeable experts on the history of Lourdes. René Laurentin has devoted some twenty volumes to careful, scholarly study of the events that took place in Lourdes some 120 years ago. In the following pages, he has made good use of the rich and solid material contained in this documentation. There is no fictionalizing in this account. Names, events, and conversations have been scrupulously drawn from authenticated documents, which the author himself has studied carefully and critically. In short, this is the book to read if one wants to meet the real Bernadette, to examine her deeds and authentic words, and to be open to the lessons of her life. That life, right up until her death, was wholly inspired by the message that she received from the Virgin Mary.

Another attractive feature of this moving and authentic account will be quickly noticed by the reader. It is written in a clear, concrete and brisk style. Instead of lengthy, protracted phrases we find simple, straightforward sentences packed with meaning; we find much to contemplate in them. There are also many lifelike details noted succinctly. The result is a vibrant story in which we discover once again the freshness and candor of the little seer of Massabielle as well as the astonishing strength of character of the young nun that she later became.

Bernadette Soubirous was beatified less than fifty years after her death, and canonized on December 8, 1933, only eighty-nine years after her birth. Among all the people to whom the Virgin Mary appeared during the nineteenth and twentieth centuries, only she and Catherine Labouré share this singular honor of such early canonization.

Bernadette lived a life of evangelical holiness that
was extraordinarily pure, simple and self-effacing. In the
last thirty years or so, we have seen an increasing number
of historical, theological, and interdisciplinary studies
about her. They have brought out more and more clearly
one trait of her character: a lowly and imitable holiness in
a person where nature and grace lived in the closest
harmony. She is a saint within our reach, a saint for our
times. She bears witness to the message that the Church
must embody today. For the Church, like Bernadette, is
summoned to live out a mystery of service and poverty
grounded in hope.

Readers will find all that and more in this book,
which I am pleased to introduce to them on the one
hundredth anniversary of Bernadette's death. Thanks to
the soundness of its information, the simplicity of its
presentation, the warmth of its style, and the depth of its
spiritual message, we shall be able to celebrate this
anniversary more intensely in our own lives. It is indeed
the best book one could ask for to celebrate this
occasion.

It is my fondest hope that many Christians will read
this book and ponder what it has to say.

† H. Donze
Bishop of Tarbes and Lourdes
Tarbes, February 11, 1978

Prologue

Who is Bernadette?

Bernadette Soubirous, the seer of Lourdes, died at the age
of thirty-five on April 16, 1879, twenty-one years after the
apparitions of the Virgin Mary to her in 1858. She died in
the convent of Saint Gildard in Nevers, France, after living
the life of a nun for thirteen years.

She alone had seen the Virgin Mary in the grotto. It
is thanks to this urchin alone—poor, uneducated and
disdained—that the shrine of Lourdes was established
and is now visited by four million visitors and pilgrims
each year.

At the news of her death people flocked to see her
in her casket, though she had gone to Saint Gildard to
hide herself away. Today in Nevers, crowds of people still
file past the reliquary where her body lies in state. It was
exhumed intact after her beatification on August 5, 1925,
which took place less than fifty years after her death. Pius XI
canonized her eight years later on December 8, 1933,
the feast of the Immaculate Conception. If she had been
still alive, she would have been 89 at the time.

Since then she has never ceased to display her
importance. It lies in a new type of holiness that the Holy
Spirit enkindled in the nineteenth-century Church: a
holiness that is wholly and purely evangelical.

And yet she is the most secret of the saints, as many
like to point out. In saying this, they are not thinking so
much of the "secrets" that guided her life. Instead they
are thinking of the private, hidden quality of her holiness,
a holiness devoid of notable deeds, great writings and
human triumphs. Hers is a holiness of the poor.

The secret of this holiness escaped Bernadette's own
mistress of novices, a remarkable woman who was holy in
her own way. She did not want to hear any talk about
Bernadette's canonization. Do we have a better chance
than she of grasping Bernadette's secret? Yes, I think we
do; but only if we proceed Bernadette's way. And her way
is the way of simplicity.

Bernadette in 1861/62. Photo Bernadou.

She herself once said: "The Passion touches me more
when I read it than when someone explains it to me" (L 576).
And to would-be historians of Lourdes she offered
this advice: "The simpler one writes, the better it will
be....In trying to dress things up, one only distorts them"
(L 550 and 576).

Her life, devoid of artifice and studied introspection,
prompts us to avoid commentary and to simply report
her deeds, actions, and words, staying as close to the
authentic documents as possible. That is the best chance
we have of revealing her secret, which is a secret of
transparency.

The Holiness of the Poor

The life of Bernadette is a perfect illustration of this text
in the Gospels: "Father, Lord of heaven and earth, to you
I offer praise; for what you have hidden from the learned
and the clever you have revealed to the merest children"
(Mt 11:25; Lk 10:21-22). This light, hidden from the
learned and the clever but revealed to the merest
children, shone on Bernadette. The more clear-eyed
people perceived this light very quickly.

At the time of the apparitions, it was perceived by
young Antoinette Tardhivail, who could not pursue her
Carmelite vocation because of her poor health. Antoinette
made this discovery in the little town where the
Soubirous family lived, poor wretches with a bad
reputation:

> Her parents are very poor...as poor as our
> Lord was on earth. And it is on this child
> that Mary has cast her gaze in preference
> to all the rich young people. Now, at this
> moment, they envy the lot of her whom
> they might otherwise have regarded with
> disdain; and they count themselves
> fortunate to be able to embrace her or to

touch her hand (Letter, March 29, 1858, D5, p. 77).

Four years later (January 18, 1862), the bishop drew the same conclusion without ever having read the above letter. In the official letter in which he recognized the authenticity of the apparitions, he wrote:

> What sort of instrument is the Almighty
> going to use to communicate his merciful
> designs to us? Once again it is what is
> poorest and most fragile in the world: a
> child of fourteen...born...of a poor family.

Bernadette herself wrote the same thing at the moment when she became consciously aware of her vocation. In a private prayer to the Queen of Heaven she wrote:

> How happy my soul was, good Mother,
> when I had the good fortune to gaze upon
> you....Yes, you stooped down to earth to
> appear to a mere child....You deigned to
> make use of the most fragile thing in the
> world's eyes (ESB, p. 187).

The one to whom Bernadette addressed this prayer should not have had any trouble recognizing herself in it. For she herself has said:

> God who is mighty has done great things
> for me. For he has looked upon his servant
> in her lowliness; all ages to come shall call
> me blessed (Lk 1:49.48).

It is the glow of this verse from the *Magnificat,* the canticle of the poor and lowly, that shines through the day-to-day life of Bernadette.

Part I

Lourdes
1844-1866

Bernadette wearing the capulet she wore
at the time of the apparitions (1358)
and holding the rosary she used then.
(Photo taken in 1861/62.)

Mill district: below, Savy.

Chapter 1

Bernadette's Childhood
1844-1858

Bernadette Soubirous was born on January 7, 1844 in
Boly, the next-to-last of five mills spaced some meters
apart along the meager brook of Lapaca, lying between
the huge crag capped by the chateau-fortress, the hilly
meadows and the woodlands rising gently towards
Bartrès.

A Love Marriage

There was joy in the mill. Bernadette was very much a
wanted child. Her birth was the crowning touch to a
marriage of love which had come about as the result of a
calamity. Here is the story behind it.

On July 1, 1841 Justin Castérot, the miller of Boly,
was killed in a cart accident on the Pouyferré road. His
widow, Claire, stood before the flour-sprinkled corpse. It
was time to give serious thought to her predicament. She
had four grown daughters and two young children in the
mill, whose wheel had now stopped turning. The dead
man had thought of himself as the mill's proprietor, but
he was nothing of the sort. These uneducated people did
not in the least understand a complicated situation. One
thing was clear: their obligation to pay an annual *fiou* of
130 *francs-or*.

The eldest daughter, Bernarde, aged 19, would have
to be married off quickly to some bachelor in the guild.
The widow Castérot made overtures to François
Soubirous of the Latour mill, who was still single at the
age of 34. He did not require a lot of coaxing. He came
readily to the mill, smiling and affable. But there was no

progress as far as the marriage was concerned. What was going on behind that amiable but stubborn forehead?

Finally it became clear. The one who interested François was not Bernarde but her younger sister, Louise, with her blonde hair and blue eyes. When he was forced to acknowledge this anomaly, François avoided offering any reasons based on affection or love. They had no place in the mill trade of nineteenth-century Lourdes.

"Louise is a better housekeeper," argued François.

The evidence was all to the contrary. Bernarde was a woman with a good head and an air of authority if there ever was one. Louise was only 17. She was too young. It would not be proper to marry her off before the eldest. François offered no reply to these arguments. He just sat there, smiling wearily. They would have to concede to him after all, because he would marry Louise or no one.

A Birth

The wedding took place on January 9, 1843 and Bernadette was born on January 7 of the following year. The next day François, proud but awkward, carried the infant to the town hall, as was the custom. The baptism took place the day after that, January 9, her parents' first wedding anniversary.

Bernadette was baptized in the old granite baptistery where inhabitants of Lourdes are baptized even to this day. She cried during the ceremony. Was it perhaps a presentiment of the strange promise she would be given later: that she would "not be happy in this world"? Another symbol points in the same direction. The most familiar noise to her in those first years was the sound of the millstones and the grain being ground. On her deathbed she would identify herself with the latter: "I have been ground in the mill like wheat."

The festive celebration of January 9, 1844 left this simple memory, recorded much later in the *patois* (dialect) of Lourdes:

*Uo tisto de crespèts, è bouteilles de pichè
sus era taoulo. On fit une ronde.*

It is easy enough to picture the scene: The people
around the table, and on it a big basket *(tisto)* of fritters
(crespèts) and large bottles that can hold from two to
three liters *(bouteilles de pichè).*

The Heir

Five women watched over Bernadette's cradle, ranging
from Grandmother Castérot to little Aunt Lucile, age 4.
The person in charge was Bernarde, "the heir." For
according to the custom in the county of Bigorre, the
firstborn, whether male or female, bore this title and this
honor. It did not matter whether there was any
inheritance or not. The opinion of the firstborn prevailed
over that of the younger children, both the males and the
females.

Bernadette, too, was born "the heir." In that capacity
she would always remain conscious of her duties to her
family.

The love which surrounded Bernadette's infancy
remained with her throughout her life. It was one of
those deep roots that grace knows how to use to fashion
saints.

Her mother, Louise, was gentle and patient. With her
happy marriage she had usurped her sister's privilege,
and she felt somewhat abashed by it all. She willingly
shared her baby without recriminations.

"She knew me as well as she knew her mother," said
Aunt Bernarde proudly.

But the touchstone for Bernadette was the silent,
smiling man of the mill, her father, who was proud of his
firstborn. In the eyes of the new heir, the royal image of
her infancy was his white-powdered beret and his eyes
gazing on her tenderly. (At that time, François Soubirous
still had both his eyes intact.)

Thus a deep sense of security took root in Bernadette. It would remain with her, indestructible, in the face of blasts that would have shattered rock. Indeed the crises could have been fatal for her if these bedrock supports had not been there, symbolizing for her another and deeper reality that was evoked each evening by the murmer of unpolished voices before sleep came: "Our Father, who art in heaven..." It was the time of day when the noise of the millstones had ceased and the gurgle of the brook gradually arose amid the deepening silence.

Bernadette did not know that her name, Soubirous, means "Sovereign." But a sovereign image, that of God, inhabited her childhood and her life of simplicity close to nature. It gave her that spirited dignity combined with humility which characterized her whole person.

Bartrès

Misfortune did not wait for Bernadette to finish out her first year. One November evening in 1844 Louise, again pregnant, was sitting in a corner of the fireplace. The resin candle hanging from the chimney fell on her. She awoke in flames. There was no longer any question of nursing Bernadette at her burnt breasts.

Aunt Bernarde went out looking for a wet nurse. In Bartrès, on the very hill whose slopes descend to the mill, it so happened that Marie Laguës had just lost her eldest son, Jean, eighteen days old. She readily agreed to nurse Bernadette, taking charge of her for five francs a month payable in silver or in cereal grain. Aunt Bernarde stayed up on the hill for eight days with the baby so that she might grow accustomed to the place more easily.

But Bernadette's most assiduous visitor was François. Before this, he had seldom been seen on the steep, four-kilometer path to Bartrès. Now suddenly there is grain to pick up, flour to deliver, or clients to badger and woo. Soon he begins to drop hints about taking back his

daughter. Marie Laguës resists. She has become attached
to the baby and she cannot reconcile herself to the sight
of an empty crib. But the crib in the Boly mill is empty
too. Little Jean Soubirous, born on February 13, 1845,
died on April 10.

Bernadette is weaned by December, 1845. But Marie
Laguës holds out. She will watch the baby *for free.* She
returns Bernadette only on April 1, 1846, when she is
sure that she herself is pregnant. All these dealings take
place in the slow and ceremonious forms typical of
peasant courtesy. When Louise Soubirous comes to pick
up her daughter, she brings a handkerchief as a gift for
this formal occasion. In the springtime Bernadette, now
two years and four months old, rediscovers the sound of
the millstones and the rushing water. They have now
become a danger for her as she toddles around with
curious and independent steps.

Good Times and Bad at Boly Mill

In 1848, the Castérot clan leaves the Soubirous'
household. Bernarde, seduced by Jean Tarbès, has
become a mother before the parents of her swain
authorize the marriage. Louise's mother, Claire Castérot,
moves from the mill, taking her unmarried children with
her. François and Louise are surprised to suddenly find
themselves alone in the mill, like two lovers. How free
and easy life becomes when one is not subject to glances,
constraints and counsels every minute!

Another event could not have escaped Bernadette's
notice. François Soubirous was "dressing" his millstones,
which had become too smooth. Suddenly he stops and
lets out a yell. He comes in, his hand over his face, his
left eye cut from a direct blow. The eye is lost.
Henceforth he hides his infirmity by keeping the eyelid
half shut, as we notice in photos of him, in order to spare
others the sight of this disgrace.

The Passion of the Soubirous Family

Are the Soubirous destined to relive the fate of Job?
Money is short at the mill. They find it hard to understand
why. They are working hard and—even with competition—
there are always some customers. But these good people
are just a bit too good-hearted to be good managers in
hard times. They open their doors readily to beggars,
including one Michel Garicoïts. They show compassion
for those who are insolvent, advancing them grain and
flour "until the coming harvest" without haggling.

"You will pay when you can," says Louise.

To customers who come to bring grain or pick up
flour the miller's wife serves a collation: a little wine, a
little cheese, and sometimes some fritters like those
served at the time of Bernadette's baptism. She is great at
making them. And why keep tabs on oil and flour when
there is so much of it? So the atmosphere is gay and
animated, but the returns are poor. The general
atmosphere drives away the "serious" clientele and
attracts the "bad" customers: those who don't pay. It gets
harder and harder for the Soubirous to pay their bills
when they fall due.

In 1854, the year that Bernadette turns 10 and that
Pius IX defines the dogma of Mary's Immaculate
Conception, the family must break up their household.
Bernadette leaves the happy mill of her early childhood.

The furniture is transported to the Laborde home.
The father begins to look all around for precarious jobs
in order to win bread for his four children. For after
Bernadette, Louise had given birth to three more
children: Toinette (1846), Jean-Marie (1851), and Justin
(February 28, 1855).

No longer a miller, François had become a *brassier,* a
"day-laborer" who hires out his arm *(bras)* and is paid for
his brute strength. The average daily pay for such a man
was 1.20 francs, less than that for a horse or a mule.
Rental of the latter had risen to 1.55 francs per day.

According to statistics in the *Indicateur des Hautes*

Pyrénées (Paris 1856), a family of five needed an annual income of at least 523 francs for their bare subsistence. There were six in the Soubirous family. Counting Sundays, feast days, holidays and days without work, François' wages are far below the mark.

Louise, too, goes out to work, doing housekeeping, washing, and work in the fields. Bernadette takes care of Justin. When he is hungry and cries, she carries him to his mother out in the fields. There, in the shade of the bales, his mother offers her breast and the baby sucks what milk is left in the ill-nourished woman who is dried out by her harsh labor under the hot sun of early summer. Of the nine children that she will bring into the world, five will not survive to the age of ten.

When Louise is unemployed, the two eldest children go out to gather wood, bones, or scrap iron. They hunt for anything that the rag-picker Letchina de Barràou might be willing to buy for a few pennies. She in turn will sell them to the big scrap dealer: Casteret. School is out of the question for Bernadette.

In the autumn of 1855, a cholera epidemic breaks out in Lourdes. It unleashes terrible attacks of diarrhea that dehydrate people in a matter of hours and reduce them to corpses.

There are eight deaths on September 23, thirty on October 10. Calamity, which prompts some human beings to take to their heels, also reveals those with a courageous heart. Father Peyramale, the new parish priest and dean who had come to Lourdes the previous March, was one of the latter. So was Commissioner Jacomet, who went everywhere to fill the breach with his friend, Sergeant D'Angla. They vie with each other in rubbing down the sick with wisps of straw, the prevailing treatment at Lourdes. Bernadette barely manages to escape the epidemic, but her health, which had become frailer since her sixth birthday, deteriorates even further. Despite the recipes of Rosine Maillet, the midwife, her asthma will never leave her.

On October 22, 1855 Claire Castérot, Bernadette's

maternal grandmother, dies. She had escaped the
epidemic, but now she is buried fourteen years after the
death of her husband. Her death temporarily restores the
financial stability of the Soubirous family. Thanks to her
frugality, the Soubirous inherit 900 francs. They purchase
a few head of livestock, hoping to start over again with
some calves, some cows, some hogs, and some stock
hatched from eggs. Investing more than they have, they
rent the Sarrabeyrouse mill on the Echez, in the village of
Arcizac-ès-Angles, about four kilometers from Lourdes.
But the contract signed by the illiterate Soubirous was
ruinous. He barely manages to stick to it for one year. At
the first expiration date of the contract they are forced to
set out again. François can no longer nurture the foolish
hope of ever renting a mill again.

They sink lower and lower. Their affection for one
another is put to the test by the incontestable reality of
their material situation: "Too many mouths to feed," as
Bernadette would put it (H2, p.30, note 85).

They must take stock of this real situation if they are
to survive.

Cabaret Servant

During the winter of 1856-1857, the Soubirous resign
themselves to the idea of separating from their first
"mouth to feed." Bernadette's godmother, Aunt Bernarde,
takes her in as a little servant girl. Bernadette will help
take care of the house and the cabaret that Bernarde
inherited from Jean Tarbès, her first husband. It is
situated on the corner of the Rue de Bourg and the Rue
du Baous.

Bernadette looks after her cousins, does the wash,
mends the clothes, does the needlework at which she
excels, and works at the counter. She docilely submits to
the firm authority of Aunt Bernarde, who runs things with
a stick when she has to; but Bernadette is inclined to
display the same generosity that characterized her parents

when they lived in the Boly mill. Her generosity is
stronger than her exemplary docility. She has a knack for
filling the pewter measuring cup on the counter of the
cabaret in such a way that a gulp was left at the bottom
after she filled a bottle. And she would say to her friend
Jeanne-Marie Caudeban (who tells the story) or to others:
"Take a drink of that, Marie!"

In Lourdes wine was relatively rare, and it was
regarded as a tonic or a marvelous remedy.

The Jail

At the start of 1857, continuing unemployment puts the
Soubirous out on the street again. They must depart from
their seedy lodging in the Rives house, leaving their good
clothespress behind, in pawn to the proprietor. Moving is
becoming easier and easier, since their load is lighter
each time. Where are they to find a roof over their heads?
Where are they to find an even worse place that will take
them in? No one wants the Soubirous any more. The last
chance open to them is The Jail, which is described as "a
foul, somber hovel," by Prosecutor Dutour in his report
of March 1, 1858.

The Jail was the scarcely habitable room of the old
prison. The latter had been abandoned because of its
unhealthiness in 1824. Jean-Pierre Taillade purchased the
building and had the bars removed from the windows,
but he had not eliminated the humidity or the stench of
poultry manure. Uncle Taillade then leased the
ramshackle building to André Sajous, his nephew and a
cousin of the Soubirous. Sajous had cut out a second
window, but it looked out on the same courtyard. Now
François comes knocking at his door. Sajous was honest
in recalling his feelings at that moment:

> I was not happy about it! They had four
> children. I myself had five. I realized full
> well that my wife, a very kind woman.

would give them some of our bread.
I used to lodge Spaniards there. They
came during the winter to do some
digging work and would sleep there on the
flagstones with their blanket over them.
Often there was no straw.

These migrants from across the Pyrenees represented
the ultimate degree of misery and poverty in Lourdes.
They were "a ragged band of Spaniards," as Zola
describes them scornfully in his journal investigating
Lourdes. The Soubirous had sunk to their level, as one
story of that period indicates.

Little Amanda Jacomet, daughter of Commissioner
Jacomet and five years old at the time, had finished her
first piece of knitting: a pair of little white stockings.
"You should give them to the first poor child who
comes along, even if it be a Spaniard," said Madame
Jacomet, who was a good-hearted woman. But the first to
present himself was Bernadette's little brother—with no
socks on his feet.
The Spaniards had left The Jail towards the end of
winter in 1856, but they would undoubtedly be back the
following winter. Thus there would be a loss of income
for Sajous. He puts off his answer until the evening and
goes to talk the matter over with Uncle Taillade, who had
bequeathed him The Jail. The conclusion seemed
inescapable: "They are out on the street. One must give
them lodging."
In the somber room, 3.72 meters by 4.40 meters
[about 12' x 14'] they do their best to squeeze in the
meager belongings of the Soubirous: two beds (three
were really needed for six people), a table, two chairs,
the children's stools, a small clothespress, and the trunk.
The latter is now big enough to hold the family's clothes
and linen, including their bed sheets. Their things are
clean. They quickly discover the vermin of the preceding
occupants.

Famine

By 1856, poverty had worsened. On August 26, the
Attorney General of Pau dispatched an alarming
confidential report to Paris:

> The wheat crop is averaging a third of the
> normal harvest. Oidium [a vine-mildew],
> which has been decimating the grape
> harvest for three years, has now reached its
> peak. Corn, which was at 13 francs in May,
> is now at 27 francs. Wheat has risen to 42
> francs.

Famine is on the horizon. The problem is doubly
insoluble, notes the report, because there is no railroad
to dispatch the wheat and no money among the poor
population to purchase it. Hunger intensifies at The Jail.
Bernadette plays at making grass soups, which nourish
only the imagination.

One day during this tragic winter, Emmanuélite
Estrade is praying in church. She is surprised by an
unusual noise alongside the catafalques. What does she
find? An unknown little boy is scraping off the wax that
had fallen from the candles, as a little rat might. Someone
who is hungry will eat anything. The little boy does not
wish to tell her his name. But during the period of the
apparitions later, on February 23, 1858, Emmanuélite will
identify the little boy as Jean-Marie, Bernadette's little
brother. Later on Jean-Marie will forget and deny this
childhood memory (H2, p. 224).

François in Prison

Right after that wretched winter is over, on March 27,
1857, the police descend on The Jail and carry off
François Soubirous as a malefactor. During the preceding
night, two sacks of flour had been stolen from

Maisongrosse, the baker. He points the finger at François
Soubirous, whom he had employed in September 1856 to
deliver flour to Luz. Maisongrosse speaks well of him:

> During the time he was with me, I had no
> reason at all to complain about his
> integrity.

But he adds:

> It is his state of misery that led me to
> believe that he might be the one behind
> this theft. (Prosecutor's Report, March 21,
> 1857)

His line of reasoning made an impression on the
police. They confiscate the half-boots of the former miller
and take him barefoot to the baker's place in order to
carry on their investigation. The prints of the robber are
nearly "the same size" as the half-boots, notes the report;
but it also points out that the setting of the nails is
different. François Soubirous added that "the shape of the
half-boots was bigger than that of the prints."

So will François be released? No, because the search
made at his home turned up a thick plank of wood.
Where did that come from? François Soubirous grows a
bit uncertain and confused. The plank had stood
abandoned for a long time against a wall on the Rue des
Petits Fossés. He had picked it up with his bundle of
sticks on returning from Bartrès. So while the flour won't
do the trick, the plank gives the police the "robbery" of
which the impoverished former miller had been
suspected. He is put in jail. The plank of wood is
"dropped off at the town hall," to be returned to its
"owner" when that party shows up. No one shows up to
claim it. Next year it will be used as the post on which
the authorities affix their notice prohibiting people from
entering the grotto as of June 1858.

In prison François muses about his family. They have
been dragged into his disgrace and now, without his daily
pay, they are even more afflicted than he by hunger.

On April 4, the Prosecutor terminates François'
pretrial detention for "humanitarian reasons," according
to his report. The investigation is dropped for insufficient
grounds. But the reputation of the Soubirous has fallen
even further. Because he is one-eyed and his affairs are
going badly, François is regarded as an idler and an
incompetent. "He drinks," add some people on the
Castérot side of the family. "It is she who drinks," say
some on the Soubirous side. There are no really solid
grounds for the accusations, but weakness and
undernourishment may at times incline them to prefer a
glass of wine to a more "normal" kind of nourishment in
order to find new heart for the tasks that face them. In
that epoch, everyone in the area shared the current idea
that wine provides strength (LHA 1, p. 77-80).

François is now regarded as a common thief. Only
two things are left to sustain his pride. First there is
Louise, spirited and unreproachful. They remain united
during their distress even as they had been in their good
times. There are never words between them. That is
admitted even by members of the two families who have
tried to set them off against each other.

And something else, something beyond themselves,
keeps them united. Through the floorboards Cousin
Sajous hears the voices of the Soubirous "bawling out"
their evening prayer in French—a language that
Bernadette does not understand. [Up to the time of the
apparitions, she spoke a dialect, or *patois*.] But through
the obscure words of the prayer she unites once again
with a presence—a presence that she accepts naturally.
And it is a support for her in the fields of Bartrès.

Bartrès / 1857

For Bernadette is back with her former wet nurse in
September, 1857. The reasons are commonplace enough.
It is the same old problem really: one too many mouths
to feed. No matter how nice it is to be all together,

having one less means a little bit more for each of the others at mealtime.

After March 1858, Bernadette's life in Bartrès would be enveloped in legend. Wondrous tales would find their way into the newspapers, told in an admiring or ironic vein. Bernadette's flock had miraculously leaped over a torrent swollen by a storm; they did not get wet from the rain, to the wonderment of all. Bernadette herself has given the lie to all these legends, much to the disappointment of her admirers.

Let us not idealize the alluring scene. For Bernadette, Bartrès was no pastoral idyll. Her meals were austere. Meat from the butcher shop appeared on the table only twice a year: on Christmas and the feast of Saint John. The regular morning and evening meal was the corn paste that Bernadette's stomach had turned against a long time ago. In her own home they would have given her wheat bread for her portion, but in Bartrès that is "the privilege of venerable, old masters."

Moreover, Marie Laguës is harsh with her former suckling. She loves Bernadette in her own way, but she has never quite forgiven her for taking the milk from her dead little son, Jean. Then she lost a second little Jean, age two, on March 1, 1850. The third little Jean, who is now in Bernadette's care, is wasting away. He will not last through the autumn.

Bernadette is not just the shepherdess and the babysitter. She is also the little maid who is expected to do all the cleaning up as well as other chores. She is docile and never sulks about her work. What hurts her the most is the fact that she had come with the understanding that she would at last be able to study her catechism with Father Ader, the parish priest of Bartrès. But the sheep graze on Thursday—catechism day—and the place of a shepherdess is with her sheep.

What was Bernadette's life like in Bartrès, where the gentle hills inspire dreams? Without a doubt it was one long solitude. But Bernadette knew how to remedy the situation by sometimes inviting along a companion,

Jeanne-Marie Caudeban, who was also a little servant girl. When Bernadette was alone, she played with her dog, Pigou, and with her lambs. She loved the "littlest ones"—one of her most distinct memories which stayed with her right up to the very end of her life.

Bernadette liked to build little altars during the month of Mary, as was customary in that area. They helped her pray. But her favorite lamb did not share her piety. He would charge her from behind and cause her knees to buckle, or else he would knock over the little altars. Bernadette could not hold a grudge against him: "To punish him, I would give him a little salt, of which he was very fond."

She loved that friendly universe, to which she brought order and peace. Little incidents like the ones mentioned above were moments of diversion amid the interminable solitude.

Her father came up to visit her, just as he had done when she was a suckling infant. One day he found her very sad in the meadow.

"Look at my sheep. Some have a green back. What is the matter with them?"

His misfortunes prompted a streak of wry humor in François: "The grass they've eaten has gotten into their back. They are going to die."

Bernadette cried, but how could one console her? The green stripe was the butcher's mark. Her sheep were indeed going to die.

Back at the house in the evening, her old nurse has got it into her head to teach Bernadette her catechism. She is trying to allay her guilt feelings for having broken her promise. But her teaching is not on a par with her good intentions. She repeats the phrases in an imperative tone, hammering them out like blows: "Say it again! Say it again!"

The words just won't stick in the head of this girl, who has never attended school. Bernadette's understanding of things come from the inside, and she cannot see any connection between these abstract phrases

and the First Communion that she yearns to make. Her
old nurse grows exasperated and ends up tossing the
catechism across the room: "Look! You are too dumb!
You will never make your First Communion!"

Father Aravant, brother of Bernadette's former nurse,
witnessed these scenes and remonstrated with his sister.
"She changed her approach for awhile...but then she went
back to her usual style," Bernadette confided to Jeanne
Védère one day (H 2, p. 58).

Without this confidential remark to her most intimate
girlfriend, Bernadette's words would have left us nothing
but comments of praise and affection for her old nurse. It
is through others that we learn of the unhappier side of
Bernadette's life.

When the Good God Permits It

Without another confidential remark to Jeanne, we would
not know something else either. This particular comment
reveals to us one of the wellsprings of her patience and
gentleness: "When the good God permits it, one does not
complain."

The remark is significant. Bernadette did not say,
"What God *wills*," when she was talking about sufferings
and injustices endured. She found peace by adhering to
her principle, but that did not keep her from looking for
a happier way out.

Both Aunt Bernarde and Marie Laguës testified to
Bernadette's gentleness and docility. But was she pious?

"Oh, like anybody else!" was the reply of Justine
Laguës to Father Servais in 1913.

"I don't recall having seen her with a rosary," said
Jeanne-Marie Caudeban, her sometime companion in the
Arribans meadow.

On her deathbed (December 12, 1878) Bernadette
herself was asked whether she had recited the rosary in
the fields of Bartrès.

"I don't remember that," was her reply.

She had forgotten a great deal. Her mother, Louise
Soubirous, noticed that from a very early age Bernadette
showed "a marked inclination towards piety" (Testimony
of November 12, 1859; D5, p. 327). She liked to decorate
little altars or shrines during the month of May, in honor
of Mary, both at home near her bed and in the fields of
Bartrès. But that was a local custom and there was
nothing singular in her practice (H2, p. 60). She owned a
rosary, which Toinette had bought for her in 1856, in
Bétharram, for two sou (A7, p. 173). She could recite the
rosary in French though she only knew the language in a
vague general way, just as many Catholics were vaguely
familiar with Latin before Vatican II (H2, p. 50). Indeed,
this rosary would be in her pocket at the time of the first
apparition, and fingering the beads was a familiar gesture
for her.

Bernadette also knew the invocation that was recited
at their evening prayer: "O Mary conceived without sin,
pray for us who have recourse to thee."

And there we have all that can be gathered from the
investigators who explored Bartrès: some to find a
miraculous origin, others—such as Zola—to pry out the
secret of a disheveled mysticism.

A Spirituality Hidden in Simplicity

Bernadette was not a mystic in the ordinary sense,
displaying some peculiar or bizarre brand of fervor. Nor
was she a mystic in the scholarly sense, displaying one of
those spiritual states that are described in manuals of
ascetic theology. And yet, for all that, she was quite
advanced in the practice of true mysticism—that is, of
union with God. She lived it in the way that poor and
lowly people do, in the way that thrilled Jesus Christ and
caused him to exclaim: "Father, Lord of heaven and earth,
to you I offer praise; for what you have hidden from the
learned and the clever you have revealed to the merest
children" (Mt 11:25).

What we are dealing with here is a quiet grace that
has left no clamorous echo in the newspapers or even in
the archives. But the priests of that region encountered it
often enough: a quiet contemplative experience evident
among the shepherds or peasants of the area.

When it comes to dealing with the holiness of the
poor and lowly, one must know how to catch the slightest
hint beneath a veil of silence or half-spoken words.
Bernadette's parents were too quiet for us to be able to
say anything about their religious experience, their
generosity of heart, or their unwavering, mutual
understanding that foiled all attempts to set them against
one another. But many visitors were sensitive enough to
catch a glimmer of all this: those who did not just come
to question and quibble but who were wise enough to
sense the reality of living beings and their circumstances.
Azun de Bernétas noted down his first impressions upon
entering The Jail on November 12, 1859:

> On entering the Soubirous home, one is
> struck by the same family air that pervades
> all the faces. Peace, innocence, and
> happiness seem to shine out from the
> placid features that typify all of them. And
> yet they are impoverished in every sense of
> the word....How happy we were in the
> midst of those blessed little ones! (D5, p. 328)

Following in their footsteps, Bernadette lived the
gospel message in the most direct way, without any
high-flown knowledge or idle chatter. Very quickly she
forgot many things. Her right hand did not know what
her left hand was doing, and she was a complete stranger
to any and every sort of spiritual exhibitionism. She
discouraged all those who sought to probe deeper than
her simplicity in trying to pinpoint her secret.

She lived her union with God at all times, amid a
dearth of words and means. She lived it in the
communion of saints—the saints on earth and in heaven,
whose presence seemed so close to the people of her

day. John the Baptist lit up the church of Bartrès from his gilded bas-relief overhead. Saint Peter did the same for the church in Lourdes. The Virgin Mary shed her gentle light on both churches.

But the holiness of Bernadette lay outside the bounds of any religious instruction. She did not even have any familiarity with the mystery of the Holy Trinity. Father Pomian realized this quickly, and with shocked surprise. Bernadette was a stranger to all reflective awareness. She lived in a spiritual night—the night of the poor little ones, of those who await the Good News while carrying out the "will of God" and enduring what he permits, as Bernadette said to Jeanne Védère when they were still children together.

Return to The Jail

Resignation to the will of God did not stop Bernadette from thinking about her plight and trying to figure out a solution. She begins to implement her thinking at the end of 1857, on her weekly Sunday trips to Lourdes, to embrace her own family.

On December 5 of that year, it is the turn of the third little Jean Laguës to die. His death reopens the wound inflicted on the heart of Bernadette's wet nurse thirteen years earlier. The atmosphere of the house grows very oppressive. The grief-stricken mother works off her emotions on Bernadette The hope of catechism lessons, put off from one Thursday to the next, is now squelched altogether. On January 3, 1858, Father Ader, the parish priest of Bartrès, says farewell to the parish house after presiding over his last baptism, his last marriage, and a final meeting of the parish council. He is leaving for Pierre-qui-Vire to pursue his attraction to the Benedictine way of life. No one yet knows who his replacement will be.

Bernadette has made up her mind. Now she must get other people to accept her decision. She informs her parents that she is "sick and tired" of life in Bartrès.

Coming from one who weighs her words so carefully, the words make an impact.

François Soubirous understands her distress. Her mother agrees. The process of leaving Bartrès gets under way quietly.

On Sunday, January 17, 1858 Bernadette is going down to Lourdes as she does every Sunday, bringing along a few potatoes, which are a real blessing. On her way out of the house in Bartrès, she withdraws into the silence of her shell when her old nurse speaks her usual parting word: "You will be back this evening, without fail."

Bernadette does not reappear that day, nor the next day, nor the day after that. It is Wednesday before she comes back, with a clear-cut and well prepared response on her lips: "Reverend Father, the parish priest, wants me to make my First Communion."

Who could contest the decision of the Reverend Father, seeing that right now there is no parish priest in Bartrès? Bernadette is now past her fourteenth birthday, and the Laguës are feeling guilty. For one last time Bernadette borrows Jeanne-Marie Caudeban's handkerchief while she washes her own. She will start for home the next day, Thursday, with her meager luggage.

Farewell to her girl friends, Jeanne-Marie Caudeban and Jeanne-Marie Garros. Farewell to her foster brothers, Zéphirin, Joseph, and Justin. Farewell to Papa Laguës, the good soul of the house. Farewell to her old nurse, whose affection always resurfaces at arrivals and departures.

Bernadette has turned her back on the Burg house. She turns left after the church and curtsies to the cross at the juncture in passing. The road she takes is not the road that has since been opened for tourists. It is a cart road, with deep, twisting ruts, that runs along the edge of the plateau before descending to the Gave river. The dark inclines of the north slope on her right do not draw her attention. On the opposite side, which does not see any sun in winter, Bernadette does not notice the sheer cliff of old rock known as the *Masse vieille* — or Massabielle in the *patois* of Lourdes. Indeed was Bernadette even acquainted with the name of that rocky recess, which was difficult of access and had a bad reputation, and which served as grazing ground for the township's herd of swine? If she was, in all likelihood it was through the old question bandied about in the area: "Have you climbed the Massabielle?" Bernadette herself had never been there.

At the end of the right fork, the road descends into Lourdes. There is the steeple of the parish church where she will at last learn her catechism and make her First Communion.

Back in The Jail, she once again discovers the poverty, the dampness, the stench, and the gloominess. But she also has the affection of her own family once again. This is the choice she has made.

The Jail—Bernadette's home at the time of the apparitions.

The first apparition; from a drawing by A. Duruy.

Chapter 2

The First Three Apparitions
February 11, 14, 18

Thursday, February 11, 1858 is a day like any other in The
Jail. The loathsome atmosphere passes unnoticed because
the occupants are used to it. It is 11:00 A.M. François
Soubirous is lying in bed because there is no work for
him that day. He is saving his strength for the next day, or
the day after that.

"Good heavens, there's no more wood!" exclaims
Bernadette.

The project is launched. Toinette wants to go too. In
comes Jeanne Abadie, called Baloum, the quarryman's
daughter. She is a big, brash girl who acts quite grown-up
and she lets it be known that she will go too.

"Not Bernadette," says May. ["May" is a patois term
for Mother or Mom.]

Outside there is mist and a drizzling rain. Louise is
afraid that the cold and dampness will not be good for
her eldest daughter's asthma. But Bernadette pleads and
insists. Feeling out of breath in the close atmosphere of
The Jail, she longs for the open air. Permission is given,
along with many words of warning and advice. May fixes
a white hood on Bernadette's head. It is a well-patched
capulet that she bought second hand on the Marcadal, the
municipal square.

Looking for Wood

The three pairs of wooden clogs echo on the paving
stones of the Rue des Petits Fossés, then on the arch of
the Baous gate that opens out on to the countryside.
There are hardly any bones to pick up in Paradise
meadow that runs along the cemetery. It is too close to
town. The three little rag-pickers descend towards the Pont
Vieux. There old Pigoune is washing some purplish guts.

"Auntie, what are you doing there? Who are you washing those guts for?"

"It's Mr. Clarens' pig. And what are you people doing here in this bad weather?"

"We're looking for wood."

"Go to Mr. La Fitte's meadow. He has cut down some trees. "

"No!" protests Bernadette. "Are we to be taken for thieves...?"

"Stay on the Massabielle side."

Three hundred meters further on, the girls cross the bridge over the canal which turns the Savy mill. It leads them into the meadow—an island between the canal and the Gave—with which they are not familiar. Nicolau, the Savy miller, comes out on his doorstep. He does not care to see the three little foragers picking their way through the freshly cut wood.

"Hey, rascals! Don't touch the wood!"

They hasten their step but retain their composure, not deigning to gather any of the branches that lie all over the ground. All over the meadow stand skeleton-like poplars, denuded of their branches.

"Let's go see where the canal rejoins the Gave," proposes Bernadette.

"And what if it rejoins it at Bétharram?" exclaims Toinette, who likes to contradict the heir.

The exploration does not take long. Two hundred meters farther on, they come to the sandy point where the Gave rejoins the channel of the mill, which is not going that day. To their left is a rocky cliff with a grotto carved out of it at the bottom. The water of the canal washes its left side. Among the rocks and moraines that ascend over the grotto the foragers see wood and bone. So far, they have found hardly anything at all.

Jeanne throws her clogs to the other side and crosses, holding her bundle of sticks on her head. Toinette follows her, holding her sticks in her hand. Bernadette is left alone on the other bank, with her asthma and her mother's cautions.

"Help me to throw some stones in the water so that I can cross!"

The two others are engrossed in their foraging.

"Pet de périclé! Cross over like we did!" shouts Jeanne.

Pet de périclé is a favorite little swear-word of her father, akin to "thunderation!" in English. Jeanne is vexed with the lazy creature who has not gathered as much as she and Toinette.

A Gust of Wind

Bernadette is looking for a way to get across. No luck.

"Then," she writes, "I came back opposite the grotto and I began to take off my shoes and stockings. I had just removed the first stocking when I heard a noise something like a gust of wind."

Bernadette looks behind her. The poplars are not moving. She bends over to take off the second stocking. The same noise again! But this time she sees branches moving directly across from her. They are the branches of a wild rosebush rooted in the bottom of a niche of some sort. It is in three meters of earth, above the right edge of the grotto. A "gentle light" brightens the dark recess and there, in the light, is a smile. Bernadette sees a wonderful girl, dressed in white. She opens her hands in a welcoming gesture that seems to invite Bernadette to come closer. Bernadette is seized with a kind of "fear," but "not to run away." On the contrary, she would like nothing better than to remain there. Bernadette fights back to make sure she is not dreaming. She blinks her eyes several times. But each time she again sees the same apparition and the same smile. Then, she tells us:

> I put my hand in my pocket, and I found
> my rosary there. I wanted to make the Sign
> of the Cross...I couldn't raise my hand to
> my forehead. It collapsed on me. Shock got

the better of me. My hand was trembling.
　　The vision made the Sign of the Cross.
Then I tried a second time, and I could. As
soon as I made the Sign of the Cross, the
fearful shock I felt disappeared. I knelt
down and I said my rosary in the presence
of the beautiful lady. The vision fingered
the beads of her own rosary, but she did
not move her lips. When I finished my
rosary, she signed for me to approach; but
I did not dare. Then she disappeared, just
like that.

There was nothing there now but the somber rock
and the drizzling rain. Happy but far from starry eyed,
Bernadette went back to her problem where she had left
it: one stocking on, one stocking off. She found her
second stocking down at her ankle and took it off. Then
she crossed the stream without any difficulty. She sat
down on one of the bigger stones among the pebbles,
right on the threshold of the grotto.

A Confidence Betrayed

Her two companions are back. Heading downstream
along the left bank, they had seen Bernadette in prayer.
Baloum had shrugged her shoulders: "It's silly to pray
there. Praying in church is quite enough!"

Now they are back with a good store of wood.
Sheltered from the rain under the roof of the grotto, they
are dancing to warm up. Bernadette does not like to see
them frisking about there.

"Did you see anything?" she asks suddenly.

"What about you, what did *you* see?"

Bernadette realizes the mysteriousness of the thing
that has happened to her. She must keep that to herself,
and so she shifts the conversation to something else.

"You jokers, you told me that the water was cold. But
I found it very mild."

Jeanne Abadie is tying up her bundle of wood.
Bernadette inspects the grotto again. She looks at the
massive cliff with its many caverns; at the pebbly ground,
brown for the most part but sprinkled here and there
with specks of red; at the bramble bush, stock still, in the
empty niche. She cannot help but ask again.

"Did you see anything?"

"What about you, what did you see?"

"Oh, nothing" (*Labets, arré* : H2, p. 181).

Toinette is becoming intrigued, but Jeanne is getting
annoyed.

"She hasn't seen anything at all. She just didn't want
to gather any wood! May will give her a good scolding!"

Jeanne loads her bundle of wood on her head and
grabs her basket of bones. She disappears into the
brushwood along the hillside, leaving the other two in
the lurch. She has no desire to put her feet into the icy
water again, preferring to climb the steep slope that will
get her to the old bridge by way of the forest road.

Bernadette and Toinette tie up their wood and take
hold of it. But Bernadette is no longer the one taking up
the rear. She gets to the top first, drops her load on the
road, and comes back to help a stunned Toinette.

"But I'm the stronger one!"

"What can I do for you?" replies Bernadette.

Suddenly Toinette becomes insistent: "Tell me what
you saw...Just me! I promise not to talk to anyone! Not
even to May!"

In a few brief words, Bernadette confides the secret
of the apparition to Toinette. It arouses in Toinette both
fear and a certain envy of Bernadette. For she is the
eldest, the heir, the one who must have stockings because
of her asthma and who gets white bread because of her
stomach.

"You want to frighten me, but I don't care now that
we are back on the road."

She hits Bernadette with a branch from her bundle.

"Silly nonsense!"

"Oh, you can believe me," says Bernadette calmly, warding off the blows.

They make their way back to the Baous gate, the paving stones, The Jail. François Soubirous is still in his bed. Meal time has passed, but May's first thought is to clean the sprigs out of the children's hair. She is obsessed by the threat of skin infection.

"Toinette!"

"You always start with me first! Do Bernadette first!"

Bernadette is off in the passageway, eating her portion of bread. The sight enrages Toinette. As she herself put it:

> Something was driving me to tell what Bernadette had said to me. So three times I went "hmm", as if I was trying to clear my throat. My mother said: "Why are you doing that? Are you sick?" No, I said, but I was going to tell you what Bernadette told me (LHA 2, p. 111).

Then she blurted out: "Bernadette saw a white girl in the grotto of Massabielle."

"Pràoube de you ('Oh, poor me')," exclaimed May. After the evictions, the failures, and the prison term, what misfortune lay in wait for them still? She gathered her remaining reserves of composure to question Bernadette: "What did you see? Tell me! What did you see?"

A Taste of the Stick

The words stuck in Bernadette's throat: "Something white." The stick for beating the bedclothes is applied to the two sisters, but not as hard to the fragile body of Bernadette.

"You didn't see anything but a white rock. I forbid you to go back there."

The father, still stretched on the bed utters a sententious remark that embodies his dream of maintaining his personal pride against all odds: "There has never been anything that anyone could say against our family. You are not going to start something."

Neither the father nor the mother understand a thing. But what is going on with Bernadette?

"We must pray," says Louise. "Perhaps it may be the soul of some relative in purgatory," she muses.

Jeanne Abadie enters. She is going to negotiate the sale of the bones they have gathered, for the celebrations of Shrovetide are almost upon them. Toinette gathers up the pile of bones they have been storing for this eventuality. Fortune smiles on them. Letchina gives them twenty sou (1 sou equals 5 cents) for the lot. Of this amount six sou (30 cents) is paid for the basket of bones collected that morning. It purchases a pound of bread, which the girls bring back to share in The Jail. There is no more talk about what happened earlier in the day.

A Dream?

That evening the family prays before the fireplace, in which the wood collected that morning is now burning. Bernadette is deeply stirred. A profound sense of peace invades her and she begins to weep. Her mother tries to question her, but what is there to say? Troubled, Louise goes to the next floor to take counsel with Romaine Sajous. The two women come back and question Bernadette in the semi-darkness by her bed. Their conclusion is: "It's a dream...an illusion. She must not go back to Massabielle again."

Do Not Go Back There!

On Friday, February 12, Bernadette feels drawn to the grotto. That is out of the question.

"Get back to work," replies her mother.

Bernadette obeys. She does not say any more about it that day or the next day. She is on the way to forgetting the whole matter, hopes her mother.

In the Confessional / February 13

Saturday evening Bernadette enters the confessional in the nearby church, where Father Pomian is hearing the regular weekly confessions. Opening the grill in the semi-darkness, he is hit with a strange admission in *patois:* "I saw something white, in the shape of a lady."

Without showing any interest, he lets the child talk, and he is astonished by the coherence of her remarks. One feature, in particular, strikes him: *"Coumo u cop de bén* ('like a gust of wind')." He suddenly thinks of the "gust of wind" of Pentecost, as reported in Chapter 2 of the *Acts of the Apostles.* Where did this child get such an idea? Where did she pick up these words, which are really beyond her?

Nevertheless Father Pomian does not attach any real importance to her disclosure. A thought comes to him which he will later describe as an "impulse from God." He says to Bernadette: "May I speak to Reverend Father (Dean Peyramale) about this?" Bernadette says yes, astonished by the priest's deference to her. That very evening Father Pomian meets Dean Peyramale on the Argelès road and apprises him of this minor matter. "We must wait and see," is all that the Dean has to say. And he moves on to talk of other matters.

Holy Water and a Big Stone / February 14

However, the report has spread among the pupils in the "poor children's class" at the hospice school run by the nuns. Toinette and Jeanne have talked. At the end of High Mass on Sunday, February 14, a project takes shape in the

minds of the little girls in patched dresses. Feeling a
mixture of enticement and fear, they determine to go see
what Bernadette saw.

Louise gives a flat ' no," then sends them off to see
François. He is working on the common field, taking care
of the horses in the stable of Jean-Marie Cazenave. The
latter man, called Ganço, runs the stage-coach line to
Bagnères.

"No," replies François Soubirous curtly, and he goes
on with his work.

But the little girls have found an ally in his boss. "A
lady with a rosary—that can't be anything bad," says
Ganço.

François gives in, but with certain reservations: "I'll
give you only a quarter of an hour."

"Oh, of course we'll be back for Vespers."

Back at The Jail, Louise has another objection: "What
if it is something bad there!"·

"We are going to bring some holy water."

The children take the route of February 11 as far as
the Pont Vieux. But instead of entering the island by way
of the mill, they climb the forest road. At the point where
it climbs above the grotto, the children split into two
groups. The smaller ones rush ahead with Bernadette; the
bigger ones tarry. They are afraid, but they affect disdain
before the younger ones.

Bernadette descends the steep, slippery slope like a
shot. The others find her there on her knees, but not out
of breath.

"How fast you ran!"

Bernadette is not listening. She has taken out her
rosary and is kneeling in prayer. The others are standing
around her. At the second decade of the rosary
Bernadette's face changes.

"Guêrat-la! ('There she is')...her rosary on her
arm...She is looking at you..."

Bernadette's companions see nothing. Bernadette
takes the vial of holy water handed to her by Marie Hilo.
She sprinkles vigorously in the direction of the

apparition, adjuring her "to stay if she comes from God, to go away if not."

"But the more I sprinkled, the more she smiled; and I kept sprinkling until the bottle was empty."

Bernadette has grown pale. She does not seem to see or hear her companions. Standing at the bottom of this gully, in a cul-de-sac with the channel behind them and the mysterious craggy rock in front of them, they feel their uneasiness growing. But Bernadette seems happy, and the sight of her inspires peace.

Suddenly something comes hurtling down the rocky cliff. It seems to shatter on the pebbles, quite close to Bernadette, and bounce into the Gave. There are splashes here and there in the water. Panic takes hold. Toinette, Pauline, and Marie flee, shrieking loudly. They think that they are being pursued. On the opposite bank a passerby hears them shouting: "It's following us!"

The more courageous ones do not want to abandon Bernadette. They are trying to drag her away. But Bernadette does not seem to hear a word. She resists their efforts, and she is unbelievably heavy.

On top of the cliff Jeanne Abadie also gives way to fright at this point, for she is responsible for the panic and the shrieking below. To assuage her own fears she had gotten the idea of creating a little fright herself by balancing a stone "as big as a hat" on top of the cliff. It had tumbled down into the midst of the group below.

The strength of Nicolau, the operator of the Savy mill on the canal, is needed to budge Bernadette. Able to toss sacks of flour around expertly, he is astonished at the inertia of this little girl. She is so small yet so heavy. Her paleness and her smiles make a deep impression on him. Is she really that heavy, or is he simply losing his strength? All along the way she seems to see something. Her eyes are "glued above."

"I put my hand over her eyes and tried to get her to bend her head, but she would raise her head again and reopen her eyes with a smile" (H 2, p. 269).

Nicolau manages to get her to his mill with great

difficulty. The girls who ran away have arrived at their
homes. Rumor grows in Lourdes. Some people hasten to
the Savy mill, including Louise with stick in hand. This is
definitely the end. Bernadette will never go to that grotto
again!

Extravaganzas?

When Bernadette goes to school the next day, Shrove
Monday, she is greeted with this rebuke from the
Superior, Mother Ursule Fardes: "Have you finished with
your carnival extravaganzas?"

When Bernadette leaves school that day, Sophie
Pailhaisson is waiting for her. Sophie is a disagreeable
woman in her forties. She had asked Sister Anastasie, the
sternest of all the teachers and "detested" by the children,
to point out to her the chit of a girl who was putting on
"comedies" in the grotto. Sophie was a strict moralist at
heart and she wanted to give the culprit a lesson.

"Look, there she is, the brat," says Sister Anastasie.

A hard slap lands on Bernadette's cheek.

"You rascal, you! If you go back there again, you will
be locked up" (H 2, p. 291).

Bernadette, her cheek burning, makes every effort to
obey and to forget—without success.

During sewing workshop that afternoon, her
companions bring her over to nice Sister Damien
Calmels.

"Tell Sister what you saw."

Bernadette tries to avoid the matter and escape: "I
don't know how to speak French."

But it is too late. The others tell the story in their
own way. Now and then Bernadette interrupts fiercely to
correct them on some point. No, there was no bouquet!
No, the apparition did not pursue them! Sister Damien is
perplexed. The excited talk turns to jibes about the pig
grotto and the lady with bare feet. Bernadette will hear
such jibes often in the days that follow.

She now regrets that she did not follow her first impulse and keep the whole matter to herself. So she wraps herself in the silence that had become a source of strength to her in the fields of Bartrès.

Is It the Soul of Élisa?

On Shrove Tuesday, February 16, Madame Milhet's interest in the grotto affair is aroused. She is an opulent woman in her fifties who came into a nice fortune when she married her former employer. Her seamstress, Antoinette Peyret, the bailiff's daughter, had told her about the grotto and the young girl who had appeared. Wouldn't that be Élisa Latapie?

The saintly death of that "Child of Mary," who had died on October 2 of the previous year, had made a deep impression on the people of Lourdes. Dean Peyramale had written a long letter about it to Bishop Laurence to "console his episcopal heart." A few hours before breathing her last, Élisa had asked to be dressed for her burial. She was to be buried in a plain dress, with her insignia as a member of the Children of Mary, but without any ribbon or lace. Now there was talk of an apparition in a white dress with a blue waist band and with a rosary on her arm. Isn't that Élisa?

"We must clear up that point," concluded Madame Milhet.

As one who employed Louise Soubirous from time to time, Madame Milhet entered The Jail triumphantly and left the same way. Tomorrow, before daylight, she would take Bernadette to the grotto.

Pen and Paper / Thursday, February 18

At 5:00 A.M. the next day Madame Milhet is knocking at the door of The Jail with Antoinette by her side.

Bernadette is still in bed. She must hurry. All three attend
the first Mass of the day. Then, in the dark, they travel
down to the Pont Vieux and head off on the forest road.
Antoinette is carrying the pen and inkstand of her father,
the bailiff. The first two apparitions made it clear that one
could not rely on Bernadette's simplicity. They would
have to get the visitor to write her own name.

Bernadette is the first to get to the grotto. Madame
Milhet arrives last. They have barely begun their rosary
when Bernadette murmurs: "*Qué-y-ey* ('She is here')."

When the rosary is finished, Antoinette hands the
inkstand to Bernadette. The seer advances under the arch
of the grotto and stops beneath an inner crevice which
communicates with the niche. Then she holds out the
bailiff's writing utensils. It had been agreed that
Bernadette was to pose a question to the apparition:
"Would you be so kind as to write down your name?"

The apparition approaches Bernadette, "gliding
through the opening," as Bernadette would describe it
later. But nothing is written on the paper.

The other two women are growing impatient. They
see nothing and they cannot even hear Bernadette's voice.
They become insistent, but Bernadette makes a sign
suggesting that they should keep quiet or perhaps get out
of the way.

At the end of the apparition they break in on
Bernadette: "But why didn't you ask her to write down
her name?"

Bernadette is astonished: "But I certainly *did* ask!"

How is it that she was not heard? The mysterious
young lady of the rock, whom Bernadette calls *Aquerò*
("that thing": see Author's Appendix) out of prudence and
respect, heard well enough. She replied simply: "*N'ey pas
necessári* ('It is not necessary')."

She had her own request to make to Bernadette, and
she made it in *patois:* "Would you have the graciousness
to come here for fifteen days?"

"*Aoué éra grácia*" is a polite formula of request, and
Bernadette was amazed that the apparition would address

a child like herself in that courteous fashion. This was the
first time that Bernadette heard her "sweet and delicate"
voice.

Bernadette had promised to come on the impulse of
the moment, without ever reflecting on the consequences.
And she had not recognized Élisa.

"And what if it was the Holy Virgin?" remarks
Madame Milhet on the way back home. Her suggestion is
swallowed up by the surrounding silence.

Madame Milhet (1813-1892).

Bernadette's sheepfold in Bartrès.

Chapter 3

The Fifteen Days of Apparitions
February 18-March 4, 1858

Trips in Secret

Since Bernadette promised and nothing has been cleared up, they must go back to the grotto! On their return to town, Madame Milhet takes charge of the whole affair. She takes Bernadette to board at her home. That way she can take Bernadette to the grotto in secret, without a lot of coming and going between the two homes. But now Louise wants to go along, and so does Aunt Bernarde. With the help of reports and rumors, there are eight people at the grotto on Friday, February 19; thirty people on Saturday, February 20; and one hundred people on Sunday, February 21.

The apparition returns, in silence. The report spreads, supported by the fervor of those who are praying the rosary in the grotto. They share the joy of Bernadette in her ecstasy, though the little seer says nothing more.

Two questions raise the atmosphere of suspense among the members of the lower class: Who is it? And what will take place on the last of the fifteen days that Bernadette is to go to the grotto? Will there be some miracle, some revelation, or some disaster? Rumors run rife.

A Police Interrogation

In the afternoon of Sunday, February 21, the little girls of the poor children's class at the hospice school come flying out of Vespers like a flock of sparrows. Callet, the rural constable, is posted on the left side of the portal. Alongside him is another gentleman in middle-class dress.

François Soubirous,
Bernadette's father.

Louise Castérot Soubirous,
Bernadette's mother.

The interrogation of Bernadette by Jacomet, in 1858.
A reconstructed scene drawn by Ferat and engraved by Dutheil in 1876.

But the gentleman is more alert and not as stiff as the ordinary members of the town's middle class. Callet points to Bernadette with his index finger: "There she is!"

The gentleman grabs her hood and says: *"Qu'em bas segui?* You will follow me." It is Police Commissioner Jacomet, with whom Bernadette's father had dealings when the flour was stolen.

Cries of sympathy go up for the little girl: "Poor Bernadette! They are going to put you in prison."

She is heard to reply: "I'm not afraid. If they put me in prison, they will let me out again."

As yet there is no police station in Lourdes. The commissioner heads for his domicile, the Cénac house, which he shares with two other men: Jean-Baptiste Estrade, the excise-tax officer, and Father Pène, an assistant curate. The house is only fifty meters away, directly across from the apse of the church. People follow them and the crowd of curious onlookers grows.

Jacomet is calm. On the threshold he turns around and stops those who are trying to enter the house. The group includes members of Bernadette's family, who have been pushed to the forefront by the crowd.

"There's nothing for you to see here!"

The door closes behind the crowd and the police commissioner settles down in his office. Bernadette's first interrogation begins. Behind her there is a discreet witness, Jean-Baptiste Estrade. He is soon joined by his sister, Emmanuélite, with the permission of the commissioner.

When Estrade arrives, Jacomet begins his interrogation, using—as always—a neutral, indifferent, cursory tone.

"Your name?"

"Bernadette."

"Bernadette what?"

She hesitates In her neighborhood she is called Bernadette Boly, after the place of her birth. Is that the name she should give him? Or perhaps he wants...

"Soubirous!"
"Your father?"
"François."
"Your mother?"
"Louise."
"Louise what?"
"Soubirous."
"No, her maiden name."
Bernadette hesitates a moment, then responds with
the eagerness of a student who has figured out the right
answer: "Castérot!"
Jacomet nods approvingly, encouraging her good will.
"Your age?"
"13 or 14."
"Is it 13 or 14?"
"I don't know."
"Can you read and write?"
"No, sir."
"Have you made your First Communion?"
"No, sir."
Jacomet is relaxed taking down his notes. He has
already gauged the child. She is simple and sincere. So
who is behind her? Who is making her go to the grotto?
Who has given her the idea that she has seen the Holy
Virgin? For the hypothesis about some soul in purgatory
has fallen by the wayside, despite all the hubbub
surrounding the death of Élisa Latapie. The prevailing
idea now is the one that came to Madame Milhet as she
was returning from the grotto on February 18: "And what
if it was the Holy Virgin?"
    That is what rumor has latched on to, and that is
what has reached the ears of the commissioner. He gets
right down to the heart of the matter, showing marked
interest. He speaks almost admiringly, to encourage talk
on Bernadette's part.
    "So then, Bernadette, you see the Holy Virgin?"
    "I do not say that I have seen the Holy Virgin."
    Has he misunderstood the matter? Is the child not
implicated in any plot or charge?

"Ah, good! You haven't seen anything!"
"Yes, I did see *something!*"
"Well, what did you see?"
"Something white."
Jacomet is getting more and more disconcerted.
"Some thing or some one?"
"That thing *(Aquerò)* has the form of a little young
lady *(damisèle)*."

The dialogue between Jacomet and Bernadette is in
the local *patois,* the only language that Bernadette knows.
Bernadette regards the apparition as a person and says
that it resembles a little or young girl. Nevertheless, as the
commissioner noted down very hesitantly, Bernadette
employs neuter, rather than masculine or feminine words,
to designate the apparition. In particular, she uses the
word *Aquerò* (accent on the last syllable). In the Lourdes
dialect the word means "that thing" (neuter). On her lips,
the word expresses peasant prudence in the face of
something unfamiliar; but also reverence in the face of an
ineffable reality that is beyond her. After all, how can she
say anything about it without other people making
derogatory or derisive remarks? That has been her
problem since the day of the very first apparition.

Jacomet, who always understands things right away, is
having a hard time getting the picture. He makes her go
back over it.

"You say *Aquerò,* that thing...And that thing did not
say to you: 'I am the Holy Virgin?'"

"*Aquerò* did not say that to me."

"But that is what people in town are saying."

Yes, that is what people are saying. Indeed that is
what is being printed in the local weekly, *Le Lavedan,* at
this very moment. It always comes out three or four days
late, and thus the February 18 issue will only hit the
streets tomorrow, February 22. But Jacomet has had his
eyes open and he knows that it will contain an unsigned
article by Bibé the lawyer. In it Bibé writes the following
in a slightly ironic vein:

A young girl, to all appearances afflicted
with catalepsy...is attracting the attention of
the populace. The topic is nothing less
than the apparition of the Holy Virgin...

Jacomet tries to get back on the track. He goes back
over the whole affair from the beginning: the handful of
bones; crossing the canal; the branches of the wild
rosebush moving *(u sarrot de brancos que anaouen,* says
Bernadette); the noise *like* a gust of wind *(coumo u cop
de bén);* and the appearance of *Aquerò.*
   "There were other girls with you when you saw (it)?"
   "Yes, sir."
   "Did they see (it)?"
   "No, sir."
   "How do you know?"
   "They told me so."
   "Why didn't they see (it)?"
   "I don't know."
   Jacomet is still careful not to contradict Bernadette.
He wants her to trust him completely and unburden
everything. Then the flaw will show up of its own accord.
   "Well, then, this girl, this young lady, was she
dressed?"
   "A white dress, tied with a blue ribbon, a white veil
on her head, and a yellow rose on each foot...the color of
the chain of her rosary..."
   "She had feet?"
   "Her dress and the roses hid them, except for her
toes."
   "Did she have hair?"
   "You see a little *(drin)* here."
   Bernadette put her fingers on her temple and traced
two symmetrical lines.
   "She is pretty *(bèro)*?"
   "Oh yes, sir, very beautiful *(beroye)."*
   "Pretty like who? Like Madame Pailhasson? Like Miss
Dufo?"
   The commissioner appreciates the local beauties.

Indeed he is an expert on the matter. Bernadette replies
with a trace of pity: "They cannot compare with her *(N'y
poden pas hè)."*
      "How old is she?"
      "...young."
      The police commissioner goes on writing. Now he
takes down information on all the people mixed up with
this apparition. His attention is drawn in particular to the
involvement of Madame Milhet. She has nothing to do
and she is a shrewd woman. She was smart enough to
make her fortune by marrying her last employer. There is
a clue worth exploring.
      "Is it this woman who tells you what you are to do?"
      "No."
      "But you are lodging with her."
      "No, I have returned to my own house."
      "Since when?"
      "Yesterday."
      "Why?"
      "My aunt did not want me to go back to her house."
      "Has Madame Milhet given you a lot of money?"
      "No money."
      "Are you quite sure?"
      "Yes, sir, quite sure."
      "What about the Sisters? Have you talked to the
Sisters about it?"
      "Yes, to Mother Superior and to the Sister in charge
of the workshop."
      "And what did they tell you?"
      "You mustn't bother about that...You dreamed it."
      They are women of good sense, thinks Jacomet. He
uses the support of these religious authorities to shake
Bernadette's assurance.
      "Yes indeed, that's right, girl. You've been dreaming."
      "No, I was very much awake."
      "You thought you saw something."
      "No, I even blinked my eyes."
      "A reflection deceived you!"
      "But I have seen *Aquerò* several times, and it was

dark. I cannot be mistaken all the time."

"And the others? They have eyes too, you know. Why didn't they see it?"

"I don't know, but I'm sure I did."

Persuasion has failed. It is time for dissuasion.

"Listen, Bernadette, everyone is laughing at you. They say that you are crazy. For your own sake, you must not go back to the grotto any more."

"I promised to go for fifteen days."

"You haven't made a promise to anyone because you've made a mistake about this! Now look here, you are going to be reasonable. You are going to promise me that you will not go back there any more!"

Bernadette is silent, but her dark eyes speak a clear message: "Since I have already promised, I cannot proclaim otherwise."

The atmosphere of the discussion changes. The police commissioner rereads what he has written down in a tone that is not at all favorable. He deliberately changes some of Bernadette's responses.

"The Virgin smiles at me," is written on his rough draft.

"I didn't say 'the Virgin,'" says Bernadette, by way of correction.

Jacomet is caught in an embarrassing situation. Since Bernadette rejects all identification and even argues when he says "the girl" or "the young lady," he is forced to write *Aquerò*. And when he refers to it, he doesn't know whether to use the masculine pronoun *il* or the feminine *elle* with the neuter word *Aquerò*. Yet Bernadette does talk about the apparition as if it were a person! He rereads several passages more than once, changing the order or content to test Bernadette. After reacting vigorously to his first few tricks, she loses all interest in the game.

"Sir, you have changed everything on me."

Periods of long silence, during which Jacomet is writing, alternate with renewed barrages of questions and intimidations. Jacomet's intelligence and his profession are on trial. No clue leads anywhere. It is neither a putup

job (by whom and why?) nor is it trickery: the girl is
sincere. It is not any desire to attract attention to herself:
she is modest. It is not a confidence game: there is no
money involved. Nor is it catalepsy: Bernadette is sane
and not a bit overexcited. He cannot get a hold on her.
Jacomet feels he is at the end of his resources, but he is
not one to let a person slip through his fingers.

He begins his interrogation again, this time
challenging Bernadette's responses.

"That is not what you told me the first time."

"Yes, it is!"

"No!"

Jacomet has donned his official cap. It gives him a
military air. The pompon on it is shaking. The tension
mounts. He bites and stings as he does when he tours the
market-place and no one dares to talk back to him.
Bernadette remains unshakeable. Jacomet is growing
more and more incensed and his voice grows louder.
Callet, his ear close to the door of the adjoining room
where Madame Jacomet is also listening, hears the police
commissioner shouting.

"Drunken sot, brazen hussy, little whore! You are
getting everyone to run after you."

"I don't tell anyone to go there."

"Oh, but you are quite content to show yourself off."

"No, I'm tired of it all."

These last words give the commissioner a terrible
idea. He starts to write feverishly at the bottom of the
third page of his official stationery. His handwriting grows
bigger on the fourth page, soon becoming twice as large
as it usually was. He has fastened on two remarks of
Bernadette: her final remark about being tired of it all
and an earlier remark to the effect that she felt an inner
compulsion to go to the grotto. He will use them to
formulate a kind of confession: i.e., that someone is
forcing her to go to the grotto. Rather than "someone,"
however, it would be better to put down her "parents."
They are responsible legally and they have every reason
not to attract the attention of the police again. (But let me

note right here that Jacomet is honest enough to
eliminate this false confession when he recopies his
rough draft after Bernadette leaves.)

While Jacomet's goose quill is jotting down the last
lines of his rough draft, the noise grows outside where a
large crowd has gathered. People are banging on the
door and the shutters; some voices are raised. Jacomet
grasps the meaning of the noise and confusion. The
crowd has pushed Bernadette's parents forward, for they
actually have the right to be present at the interrogation.
Jacomet has finished writing. Before confronting his
challengers, Jacomet makes one last effort with the girl he
has been interrogating: "Listen, Bernadette, you have put
yourself in a bad spot. I am quite willing to fix things up
between us, but on one condition. Admit that you haven't
seen anything."

"Sir, I did see something. I cannot say otherwise."

"At least promise me that you will not go back to the
grotto any more. This is your last chance."

"Sir, I promised to go there."

"Very well, have it your way. I am going to get some
policemen to take you to prison."

Jacomet gets up. Bernadette does not budge. In
actual fact Jacomet heads for the front door where
someone is knocking for him. The crowd has pushed
François Soubirous to the forefront.

"They don't have the right to interrogate her without
you!"

"Go ahead in, if you love your daughter!"

François, too, is getting mad. He does indeed love
his daughter. He will not have anyone saying that he does
not know how to defend her.

Suddenly the door opens. François finds himself face
to face with the police commissioner. He enters
courageously. But the door is quickly closed behind him,
and he suddenly finds himself alone with Jacomet. With
all his experience as a poor person, he knows that being
innocent is not enough to keep a person out of prison.
He has taken off his beret and is fingering it, not knowing

quite what to do next. He makes his claim humbly and
politely.

"I am the father of the little one."

Jacomet becomes even more amiable:

"Ah good, Father Soubirous, I am pleased to see you.
I was just on the point of sending for you, because this
comedy cannot go on any longer. You are attracting
people to your house."

"But..."

"I know everything now. The little girl is tired of the
whole thing, she told me. She has had enough of you
people forcing her to go down there."

"Forcing her? We have done everything to stop her!"

"But that is what she ended up telling me in tears,
and here it is written down on this paper by me: 'Papa
and mama are outside. You must prohibit them from
forcing me to go to the grotto. I'm tired of it all, and I
don't want to go there any more.'"

François looks anxiously at the piece of paper, akin
to the one that got him sent to prison less than a year
ago, but he cannot read a single treacherous word of it.
Bernadette is protesting vigorously, but the commissioner
keeps her out of it. Now it is between him and her father.

"Good, good, Father Soubirous! I myself would like
to believe you, but it's up to you to prove that you are
sincere. Forbid Bernadette to return to the grotto and
shelter her from all the people who are running after her.
Then the whole affair will be over."

François Soubirous is conciliatory.

"It is true that we are weary of seeing our home
invaded, and that we have done everything to prevent her
from going to that place. In giving me this order, you are
doing me a service. I will close my door to people, and
the little one will not go to the grotto any more."

François leaves, content to have recovered his
daughter. And Jacomet is happy to have landed upright on
his feet once again.

Bernadette leaves as she had entered, not a bit
shaken or beaten. The police commissioner who makes

such an impression on everyone had not intimidated her
a bit. Now she cannot help but smile over his feints, his
accusations, and his fits of anger. When back at The Jail,
Dominiquette Cazenave questions her about the
interrogation and the commissioner, Bernadette replies
with a laugh: "He was trembling. And there was a tassel
on his cap which kept going ting-a-ling."

No Appearance / Monday, February 22

The next day Bernadette is again confronted with her
own problems. In the morning she feels a strong urge to
go to the grotto. The answer is no. Bernadette tries to
obey as usual. But she feels very ill at ease because she
had promised to go to the grotto for fifteen days. No
reasons reassure her. She replies: "Then I must disobey
either you or *Aquerò*."

Bernadette is under great stress and forces herself.
Mother Superior, who had seen her led away by the
police commissioner the previous afternoon,
congratulates her on the end of her "carnival
extravaganzas." The jibes of her companions continue.
But all that is nothing compared to the inner laceration
Bernadette feels. Never has obedience weighed so heavily
on her as it does this interminable morning.

Bernadette is on her way back to school after her
meager midday meal. But as she passes the threshold of
the colonnade, an inner force brings her back to herself.
She pivots on the spot and starts for Massabielle by the
quickest possible route. She goes down through the mill
quarter of her childhood and turns left on the Pè de
Pesquè path, between the chateau-fortress and the Gave.
She is being followed by others: not only by sympathizers
but also by policemen who were watching her return to
school. Bernadette is not at ease—her disobedience
disturbs her. At the Pont Vieux she stops. Other times she
had a candle, but now she has none. Aunt Bernarde has
someone go after Aunt Lucile's.

Now Sergeant D'Angla arrives on the heels of the policemen. He shrugs his shoulders on seeing the gathering that had been so quickly improvised, and comments: "Here in the nineteenth century they would like to have us believe in such superstitions as this!"

Bernadette is in her usual place in front of the rock, but this time she is flanked by Sergeant D'Angla. He repeats the same phrases over and over, growing more and more ironic each time: "Do you see her?...Do you see her?...You see her as much as I do!"

Bernadette is silent. To those who were in the grotto the preceding days, it is clear that nothing has taken place. Bernadette finishes her rosary without any change in her countenance. No light has come to pierce the darkness, and her distress arouses sympathy. Aunt Bernarde puts out the candle and leads her off to rest at the Savy mill, as she did on February 14.

Sergeant D'Angla is triumphant: "The wings of my cap sent the apparition flying off!" The comments of the people vary. "It's a lot of foolishness," say some. "It's because of the policemen." say others. "The hour had passed," say still others. The last explanation is the one accepted by the "believers," as they are now beginning to be called.

Bernadette herself murmurs: "I don't know in what way I have failed her..."

That evening she slips into Father Pomian's confessional for the second time. She poses her problem of conscience to him. Prompted by some inexplicable inner impulse, he settles the matter conscientiously: "They do not have the right to stop you."

At the very same moment the authorities were deliberating about the same matter. A conference was being held by Sergeant D'Angla, Prosecutor Dutour, and Mayor Lacadé. The latter makes this observation:

The prohibition has no legal basis. Public opinion is on the side of the little girl, and the people will not fail to blame us if we

take action against her. She must be kept
under surveillance, to be sure, but it would
be a mistake to repress her.

This moderate opinion prevails. Bernadette's knotty
situation is untangled.

Seventh Apparition / Tuesday, February 23

On February 23, Bernadette is on her way to the grotto
by 5:30 A.M. The number of people at the grotto is
around 150, almost a crowd. For the first time the fancy
hats of society ladies and gentlemen are seen among the
berets and capulets of the poorer people. Even some of
the intelligentsia who meet at the *Café français*: Doctor
Dozous; M. Dufo, a lawyer and town councillor; and
Jean-Baptiste Estrade, who had been present at the police
commissioner's interrogation of Bernadette two days
before. Estrade is secretly interested in the matter, but he
is also perplexed. He is present today only because of the
insistent pleading of his sister Emmanuélite and her
friends, whose curiosity has reached a fever pitch.
Estrade himself has come only to serve as an escort, for
in this era, young ladies from good families do not go out
by themselves. He is skeptical and ironic on the trip to
the grotto, a convinced enthusiast on the way back home
afterwards. Bernadette's ecstasy captivates him completely:

> I saw Mademoiselle Rachel in the
> Bordeaux theater. She is magnificent...but
> infinitely inferior to Bernadette...That child
> has a supernatural being in front of her.

Estrade's conversion spreads the news and the
credibility of the apparition. But *Aqueró* still maintains
her silence and Bernadette still does not know her name.

Eighth Apparition / Wednesday, February 24

On Wednesday, February 24, Bernadette has a hard time
getting to "her" place amid a crowd of almost 300 people.
After her recitation of the rosary in ecstasy, something
new is added. Bernadette advances on her knees, and
then she seems to throw her face on the ground.

Her Aunt Lucile, age 18, is at her side. When
Bernadette does this, Lucile lets out a cry and faints.
Bernadette is startled. She had just prostrated herself and
kissed the ground at the request of the apparition.

Bernadette returns to the reality around her to say:
"Auntie, don't be troubled." But the apparition is gone.
Today she had uttered a new word and repeated it:
"Penitence!" She said: "Pray to God for the conversion of
sinners." Then she had asked Bernadette: "Go kiss the
ground as a penance for sinners."

Muddy Water / Thursday, February 25

On February 25, people begin to flock to the grotto
around 2:00 A.M. For there are not too many spots where
one can get a good view of what is going on. All night
people knock on partitions and shutters, alerting their
friends. When the seer arrives at the grotto, there are 350
people there.

Bernadette recites the rosary in ecstasy as usual.
Then, after handing her candle and her white capulet to
Éléonore Pérard alongside her, she repeats the action that
had been interrupted by Aunt Lucile the day before. On
her knees she crawls up the sloping ground that leads to
the back of the grotto. Now and then she kisses the
ground. Her effortless agility on the pebbly ground is
surprising. People make room for her. They are watching
to see what will happen.

Bernadette arrives beneath the open crevice of the vault, a vertical chimney that communicates with the niche where the apparition is. Bernadette stops. Her lips are moving. But as is always the case in these conversations that open out on another world, no one can hear the sound of her voice. Bernadette seems to give her assent. Then suddenly she is coming back out, still on her knees, and moving towards the Gave. There something brings her to a halt. She goes back towards the niche and heads in the opposite direction towards the very back of the grotto, standing this time. At the point where the bottom of the vault joins the sloping moraine floor, Bernadette bends down. Her eyes seem to be searching for something or other. Disturbed, she comes back out again, looks once more at the inner cavity, and then goes back in. This time she bends down to the ground, reluctantly regards the muddy soil saturated with water, casts an embarrassed glance at the cavity, scrapes the soil with her right hand, and forms a little hole. She then draws a kind of reddish mud out of the hole, brings it to her face, rejects it with disgust, and begins again. She would really like to drink this filthy water, but her repugnance is too great. She manages to do it only on the fourth try. Then she eats a few of the round-leafed herbs growing at the back of the grotto: golden saxifrage.

What in heaven's name is she doing? The onlookers don't understand a thing. When she comes back out, her face all dirty, there is consternation.

"She's crazy!" some whisper.

Estrade's enthusiasm had drawn some of his friends to the grotto with him. They want to see this rival of the famous Rachel (who had died the preceding month). Now they do not conceal their disappointment. Elfrida Lacrampe, the daughter of the innkeeper, explodes with the language of her father's grooms when she gets angry. She is angry now: "As far as Rachel is concerned, you have brought us out to see a little craphead!"

Estrade does not know what to say. His fervor has collapsed. He admits his plight: "I am completely at a loss. I don't understand it at all." There will be plenty of debate that evening at the *Café français,* and he will cut a very bad figure.

To those who ask her about it, Bernadette offers this explanation:

> Aquerò told me: Go drink at the spring
> and wash yourself in it. Not seeing any
> water, I went to the Gave. But she
> indicated with her finger that I should go
> under the rock. I found a little water, more
> like mud: so little that I could scarcely cup
> it in my hand. Three times I threw it away,
> it was so dirty. On the fourth try I managed
> to drink it.

"But why did she ask you to do that?"
"She didn't tell me."
"What about the herb that you ate?"
Bernadette has no reply.
"Do you know that people think you're crazy to do things like that?"
"For sinners," is Bernadette's only reply, repeating what she heard while she was in her state of ecstasy.

Sinners and sin: is it such a serious matter as all that? The look and tone of Bernadette opens new horizons.

In the afternoon some people return to the grotto. They look at the hole that Bernadette dug. It is as "big as a souptureen." Éléonore Pérard plants a stick in the basin of muddy water and detects the gurgle of flowing water. Others try to take a drink as Bernadette did. The more they dig out the hole and draw off water, the more the water spouts up and the clearer it becomes. A patch of mud that is turning into pure water: one begins to grasp the message demanding the conversion of sinners.

Two bottles of the water go back to town that day. Jeanne Montat brings one to her sick father. "He must drink some of this water," she thinks to herself.

The other bottle is brought back by the son of the tobacconist, who wore a patch over his eye. In the days

that follow, Jacquette Pène, the sister of the assistant
curate (Father Pène), observes that the boy is no longer
wearing the patch. She had seen him drawing water from
the hole.

A Session with the Imperial Prosecutor

That same evening a police agent presents himself at The
Jail: "The Imperial Prosecutor requests Bernadette
Soubirous to present herself at his home this evening at
6:00 P.M."

François Soubirous is at the big market in Tarbes, to
which he has driven one of Cazenave's coaches. What is
Louise to do? In tears she appeals to Cousin Sajous, who
is working at the Ger quarry. He hurries home and dons
his Sunday suit.

The prosecutor lives 300 meters away in the Claverie
house, on the Rue Marcadalouse. (Today that house is the
rectory of Lourdes, and the name of the street has been
changed to Rue de Bagnères.) When they get there, the
prosecutor casts a suspicious glance at the fellow
accompanying the two females.

"Are you her father?"

"No, her uncle, and the master of the house where
she stays."

"Bernadette, you and your mother come in. You, wait
here!"

Sajous is blocked from entering and the door is
·closed on him.

The interrogation is conducted according to the
rules, as was that of the police, but the pace is not as
brisk. Prosecutor Dutour is a meticulous intellectual. He
does not have Jacomet's feline resourcefulness. He seeks
to impress the culprit by taking refuge behind his office.
But neither the trappings of justice nor the solemnity of
the inkstand intimidate Bernadette.

The prosecutor starts off well enough. He is aloof,
methodical, authoritative. But Bernadette's answers upset

his plans and he loses the thread of his argument. It is
the one fault of this irreproachable man, pitilessly noted
in the reports of his superiors and evident in his own
drafts. Bernadette laughs when she sees him missing the
hole in his inkstand. He has exhausted every means to
uncover fabrication, over-excitement, self-interest, and the
other classic motives. He tries to finish the business.

"You are going to promise me not to go back to the
grotto any more."

"I promised to go there for fifteen days."

"A promise made to a lady that no one sees isn't
worth anything. You must stay away."

"I feel a great deal of joy when I go there."

"Joy is a bad counselor. Listen instead to the Sisters,
who told you that it was an illusion."

"I am drawn there by an irresistible force."

"And what if you are put in prison, what will you do
then?"

"Oh, if I can't go, then I won't."

Mr. Dutour makes a last attempt at intimidation.

"Go tell the commissioner to come for the little girl
and have her put in prison."

May suddenly bursts out sobbing. She has been
standing beside Bernadette for two hours, and now she is
tottering. Bernadette is standing too. The prosecutor takes
notice.

"There are chairs. You can sit down."

His tone suggests the condescension and disdain that
will show up in his next report. Bernadette senses the
undertones and blurts out immediately: "No, I would soil it."

So while May flops into a chair pushed over to her
by Madame Dutour, Bernadette settles herself "on the
ground like a tailor."

People are now banging on the shutters. Sajous and
his friends, who have had time to down a few drinks in
his cousin's café across the way, are beginning to make a
scene. The prosecutor begins to tremble. His hand cannot
find the hole of his inkstand.

After a few final words of intimidation, the two

women are released. The interrogation has not been a
success. Later the prosecutor will destroy the disordered
notes of his draft. Meanwhile Bernadette and her mother
are taken across the street for a final drink at Sajous' café.

It is almost nine o'clock when Bernadette gets back
home to The Jail. Dominiquette Cazenave eyes her when
she enters.

"So, did you confess?"

"Yes, I told the truth. They speak lies."

She simply cannot understand the tricks and
contradictions of those gentlemen. She asks laughingly:
"When a person doesn't write well, does he make
crosses? The prosecutor kept making crosses (i.e.,
scratching out things on his notes)."

"What a child you are!" exclaims her mother.

Bernadette's account will be inflated to fantastic
proportions by the populace. The trembling of the
prosecutor will become St. Vitus' dance. His crossings out
will become big crosses that he felt compelled to put
down on his paper. And that evening, people will assure
their listeners, the candles in his house lit up by
themselves. Bernadette will have nothing to do with this
mythology.

No Apparition / February 26

On the morning of February 26 she finds herself again in
the same situation she had been in on February 22, after
her interrogation by the police commissioner. She is
forbidden to go to the grotto. The prohibition comes
from higher up. But today a group of people are waiting
at her door. Bernarde Castérot, conscious of her duties as
the eldest, has come to The Jail. She sits on the table,
perplexed. Bernadette looks at the family authority,
waiting for her to say something.

"If I were in Bernadette's place, I would go!"

Without a word Bernadette takes down her white
capulet from the wall.

Today there are almost 600 people at the grotto. It
takes an immense amount of good will on the part of
everyone to get Bernadette to "her" place. She recites the
rosary. Nothing happens. She again performs her
penitential exercise for sinners. Nothing happens. She
makes a gesture of supplication. Those close to her who
are watching this interpret for the others: "Everyone, on
your knees!"

But *Aquerò* has requested nothing. *Aquerò* is not
there. Bernadette washes herself in the spring, which has
grown clearer during the night. She prays in vain. They
take her to the Savy mill, her refuge on unhappy days.
Inconsolable, she asks herself: "What have I done to her?"

The Penitential Apparitions / February 27-March 1

Aquerò is there to meet Bernadette the next morning,
February 27. The crowd is larger, despite the
disappointments of the two preceding days. One of the
new arrivals is Antoine Clarens, headmaster of the high
school in Lourdes. He has come to shed the light of his
education on this murky affair.

When Clarens gets back home, he starts to prepare a
memorandum entitled *La grotte de Lourdes.* It is for the
prefect, his friend and patron. The exercises of the seer,
who crawls on her knees and kisses the ground, have
made a bad impression on Clarens. That evening he goes
to question Bernadette. The naive assurance of the child
and her charm impress him. Without emphasis she
explains the meaning of her strange acts: "In penance,
first for myself, and then for others."

Clarens is perplexed. His "lights," so effective in
dispelling popular superstitions, cannot get any hold in
Bernadette's limpidity.

In the presence of an ever-growing crowd,
Bernadette continues her penitential exercises the next
day and the day after that. Eleven hundred and fifty
people are present on Sunday, February 28. That same

day Renault, the commandant of the constabulary forces,
comes from Tarbes to consult about measures required
by the growing crowd. For the people at the grotto are
wedged in dangerously between a sheer cliff and the
Gave River.

When High Mass is over, the warden of springs,
Latapie, grabs Bernadette by her capulet. There will be
another interrogation today, as there had been last
Sunday. This time it is conducted by Judge Clément Ribes,
the examining magistrate. The judge runs up against
Bernadette's resolve to go to the grotto "till Thursday,"
because she has "promised." He is without legal means to
stop her.

On Monday, March 1, people arrive at the grotto
around midnight. An atmosphere of quiet and meditation
prevails. Prayer is improvised on the spot. There is a
crowd of fifteen hundred people. One can see the white
cloaks of the Visens soldiers and, at the last minute, the
cassock of a priest. His name is Father Désirat, and he is
not from Lourdes. He is unaware of the fact that Dean
Peyramale has forbidden the clergy to go to the grotto.
His arrival creates a sensation and people make way for
him. Much to his own bewilderment, he finds himself in
the front row. His eyes like saucers, he sees Bernadette in
ecstasy. It left an indelible impression on him:

> Her smile passes all description. Neither
> the most capable artist nor the most
> consummate actor could ever reproduce
> her charm and grace. Impossible to
> imagine it.
>
> What struck me was the joy and the
> sadness on her face. When one succeeded
> the other, it happened with the speed of
> lightning. But...there was nothing brusque
> about it: a marvellous transition. I had
> observed the child when she came to the
> grotto. I had watched her with meticulous
> attention. What a difference there was

between the girl she was then and the girl
I saw at the moment of the apparition!
Respect, silence, recollection reigned
everywhere. Oh, how good it was there! I
thought I was in the vestibule of paradise.

First Miracle

That day there occurred at the grotto the first of the seven
cures that the bishop would eventually regard as the
"work of God." But he would do so only after long
inquiries by the episcopal commission and Professor
Vergez, M.D. (D 6, p. 250; see D 5, pp. 168-69, 263-64, 357).

In the middle of the night Catherine Latapie, called
Chouat, sets out for Lourdes. She is nine-months
pregnant. She takes her two youngest children with her
on the trip to the grotto, which is seven kilometers away.
She is acting on a sudden impulse, driven by desperation.
In October, 1856 she had climbed an oak tree to knock
down acorns for her hogs. She had fallen from the tree.
The doctor was able to set the disabled arm, but two
fingers on her right hand remained paralyzed and
doubled up. It is a disaster for Catherine because she
cannot spin, knit, or do anything useful.

She witnesses the apparition with her two little ones.
Then she climbs to the back of the grotto, to the source
of the little stream of water that now flows to the Gave.
She plunges her hand into the water and feels a wave of
softness flow over her. The bent fingers have suddenly
regained their suppleness.

A violent labor pain cuts short her prayer of
thanksgiving. She murmers: "Holy Virgin, who has just
cured me, let me get back home!"

Quickly she grabs the two children by the hand and
hurries over the seven kilometers to Loubajac. When she
gets home, she goes into labor without any help and
"almost without pain." The midwife, alerted hastily,
arrives only in time to hear the first cry of the newborn

babe. It is a boy, to be named Jean-Baptiste. He will
become a priest.

A Chapel and a Procession / March 2

At the end of her ecstasy before 1,650 people on March 2,
Bernadette sets out for the rectory. She is preceded there
by some of the devout, who have gotten a message out of
her: "Go tell the priests that people are to come here in
procession and to build a chapel here."
    The devout listeners recall only the first point: the
procession. It is an urgent matter in their eyes. It
obviously is meant for the "big day," Thursday, the day
after tomorrow which will mark the close of the fifteen
days! Bernadette said nothing specific like that, but it is
obvious to these people.
    Bernadette hurries to bear this message to the
rectory, but she does not stay there long. For Dean
Peyramale immediately realizes the consequences of this
idea about authorizing processions right now. The
authorities are concerned about stopping the flow of
foolish people to the grotto, the bishop in all likelihood
would refuse to authorize such a project, and it would
bring down ridicule on Dean Peyramale. Irritation mounts
inside him, all the more because he feels obliged to
neutralize his inexplicable propensity to believe who is at
work in all this—considering all the fruits of grace
evident in his parish. The devout bear the brunt of this
interior conflict. They are met with one of the sudden
bursts of anger of which the Dean is capable in difficult
matters.
    Now Bernadette arrives with her two aunts, Bernarde
and Basile. They get a bad reception.
    "You're the one who goes to the grotto?"
    "Yes, Reverend Father."
    "And you say that you see the Holy Virgin?"
    "I did not say that it is the Holy Virgin."
    "Then who is this lady?"

"I don't know."

"So, you don't know! Liar! Yet those you get to run after you and the newspaper say that you claim to see the Holy Virgin. Well, then, what do you see?"

"Something that resembles a lady."

"Something! *Qu=ouqu'arré!*"

The dialect word sounds out like a clap of thunder. Bernadette tries to convey the request for a procession. But the situation is one of thorough confusion. She does not know that the devout have been to the rectory ahead of her and have asked for a procession on Thursday. The priest's anger rises again. He is fighting against aggression and against himself. He stalks up and down the room, repeating: "So, then! A lady! A procession!"

He looks at the two aunts, both of whom he had chased out of the Children of Mary because they had gotten pregnant before marriage.

"It is unfortunate to have a family like this, which creates disorder in the town." He casts a withering glance at Bernadette: "Keep her in check and don't let her budge again."

Aunt Bernarde has stolen away. Basile and Bernadette shrink to the size of "two grains of birdseed."

"Get out of here!"

This last remark by Dean Peyramale sounds as if he were saying: "Get thee behind me, Satan."

"You will never get me to go see Reverend Father again," says Basile when they leave. But a few steps farther on, Bernadette stops.

"Oh, Aunt Basile, we must go back! I forgot to tell him about the chapel!"

"Don't count on me any more! Really, you are making us sick!"

Bernadette locks in vain for someone to go with her. Everyone turns their back—except, in the end, Dominiquette Cazenave, the sister of the station-master for whom François Soubirous works. Dominiquette goes off to the rectory alone and arranges a meeting for later. It will take place at 7:00 P.M., when Reverend Father will have calmed down.

There are several priests at the meeting: Father Pène, Father Serres, and Father Pomian, her confessor. It is a solemn assembly indeed. Bernadette conveys the second part of her commission: "Go tell the priests to have a chapel built here" (H 5, p. 182).

But she is so deeply affected that, for the one and only time in her life, she adds a commentary on the terms of the message: "A chapel...as quickly as possible, even if it be very small."

"A chapel? Is it as it was for the procession? Are you sure of it?"

"Yes, Reverend Father, I am sure of it."

The shock and imbroglio of the morning had erased the request for a procession from the frail memory of Bernadette. Did the apparition really talk about Thursday? What words did she speak? Everything has disappeared from her mind, as the catechism phrases did when she was in Bartrès. Bernadette retains a vague idea of the procession. But she cannot in all honesty be precise about it.

"You still don't know what her name is?"

"No, Reverend Father."

"Well, then, you must ask her."

Dean Peyramale lapses into silence. The other men present pick up the conversation, raising all the questions that had come to surround the event. Father Pomian, afraid that there will be a recrudescence of folklore and local superstitions asks: "Have you heard talk of fairies?"

"No, Father."

"Have you heard talk of witches?" asks another.

"No, Father," replies Bernadette (all of this in the local dialect, of course).

"You're lying! Everyone has heard talk of witches in Lourdes."

Dominiquette has experience on the stage-coach line, so she has become quite an expert in unravelling misunderstandings due to dialect differences between one valley and the next. At this point she intervenes: "Father,

she doesn't understand you. Talk to her about *brouches.*
Sourcieros doesn't mean anything in the local dialect
here."

Father Pomian mobilizes his knowledge of the local
patois to ask his question: "What are the *paráoulos* the
lady spoke to you?"

"There is no *paráou* in there," replies Bernadette.

"What? She spoke no words! But this chapel, this
procession!"

Dominiquette interrupts again: "Father, she does not
understand you. In Lourdes people say *parólos,* not
paráoulos as they do in your valley. When you say
paráou, it means 'kneading trough' to her."

Then Dominiquette added: "Reverend Father, let her
go!"

Bernadette leaves on Dominiquette's arm, feeling
buoyant.

"I am quite content I performed my commission!"

The Vigil / March 3

On March 3 there are 3,000 people at the grotto. Clusters
of people are clinging to every nook and cranny of the
cliff and the slope. They pray for hours, but few manage
to see Bernadette. What happened that morning?
Contradictory reports circulate in town. Some say she did
see the apparition. Others say she did not.

The fact is that *Aqueró* did not appear among the
early morning throng. Bernadette left the grotto upset, as
she had on February 22 and February 26. But she came
back a little later on the footpath leading to the fort. And
this time *Aqueró* kept her rendezvous.

That evening, when Dean Peyramale returns from
Tarbes where he went to consult with Father Ribes,
Bernadette rings the doorbell of the rectory.

"Reverend Father, the lady still wants the chapel."

"Did you ask her for her name?"

"Yes, but she only smiled."

"She is having a lot of fun with you!"

The fervor and the conversions which the Dean knows to be occurring in the parish nurture hope in him. He gets the idea of asking for a sign that will erase his perplexity. In the sixteenth century the Virgin had appeared in Mexico. There she had caused the hillside to flower in the dead of winter.

"Well, then, if she wants the chapel, let her tell you her name and cause the rosebush in the grotto to flower. Then we will have a chapel built, and it will not be 'quite small' at all. No! It will be nice and big," adds Dean Peyramale, who doesn't go for shabbiness at all.

The Big Day / Thursday, March 4, 1858

The last day of the fifteen has come. It is the "big day," as everyone puts it. At 11:00 P.M. the night before, the police commissioner is at the grotto. He inspects all its cavities to make sure that no fake machinery or fireworks have been planted to ensure a miracle. He is astonished to find people there already. And they are praying!

At 5:00 A.M. he repeats his inspection. It is difficult to do because the people are crushed into every nook and cranny of the grotto. They have come from all the surrounding valleys. At 6:00 A.M. the policemen of Argelès and Saint Pè have assembled in front of the town hall. The soldiers from the fort are there too. Some people are already on guard duty along the road.

Daybreak reveals a huge crowd massed on both banks of the Gave. The red capulets of the people from Barèges mingle with the white capulets of the people from Lourdes. The chateau-fortress atop the peak, which dominates the crossroads of the seven valleys, has never looked down on so many people, particularly in this deserted spot. Estimates range from 8,000 to 20,000. (As usual, it is safer to go with the lower figure.)

The crowd is astonishingly calm. The praying has not stopped. People have put up with the crowding, the

cramping, and even with the moving back and forth that
dips the first row into the canal waters now and then.
Fortunately, it is the shallow spot where Bernadette began
to take off her stockings on February 11.

At 7:00 A.M., the usual hour in recent days,
Bernadette isn't there. Anxiety mounts. The crowd is
getting exasperated from aches and fatigue. Have the
authorities locked Bernadette up illegally? Keenly aware
of the mood of the crowd, Commissioner Jacomet, who
has been on the scene since 5:00 A.M., sends young
Tarbès to find out what is going on: ' Go see if Bernadette
is on her way!"

At 7:05 the crowd on the slope breaks into noisy
chatter: "There she is!"

Bernadette has arrived, in the company of Jeanne
Védère, her grown-up cousin. Jeanne, age 30, is the
Momères schoolteacher. Bernadette promised her that
she could be by her side during this apparition. The two
females attended Low Mass at 6:30 A.M. and left at the last
blessing for the grotto.

The crowd finds some way to move aside so that
Bernadette and her entourage can pass. The agents of law
and order merely assist the good will of the whole
assembly. In fact, Bernadette had made her own
provisions earlier. Having found her way blocked the
previous day, and having missed the apparition in the first
morning trip, Bernadette had decided to do something on
her own. That day she had climbed the winding steps of
the Rue des Espénettes to ask Ganço for assistance. He
was her father's employer, who really knew how to pack
people in when he drove the stage-coach at full speed.
That evening Tarbès, the wheelwright, had erected a
footbridge of wooden planks down at the grotto so that
Bernadette could arrive on the spot at the appointed hour
and thus not miss her meeting.

And now, the next day, she is right in her spot! But
Jeanne Védère, alas, is stopped on the far side of the
footbridge. The crowd forms right behind the seer. But
Bernadette has not forgotten her promise and so she asks

for her cousin. People hang on her every word. Jacomet and a policeman cross the footbridge and point to Jeanne, one of the many gazing enviously at the bridge.

"Are you the one?"

In the twinkling of an eye Jeanne finds herself right alongside her cousin Bernadette, as the latter had promised.

At the third Hail Mary of the second decade of the rosary, Bernadette goes into ecstasy. The police commissioner and the deputy mayor are busy taking notes in their notebooks. Jacomet is particularly diligent in noting every gesture that Bernadette makes: "Thirty-four smiles and twenty-four bows in the direction of the grotto." The crowd imitates her Signs of the Cross. At the end of a half hour, Bernadette goes under the roof of the grotto to the place where she holds conversations with the apparition. Her lips move, but no sound filters out to the crowd around her. For two minutes she remains there, completely happy. During those two minutes alone, according to Jeanne Védère, Bernadette smiles eighteen times, grows sad for three minutes, and then brightens up again. Afterwards Bernadette bows, returns to her original spot, and takes up the recitation of the rosary for another fifteen minutes. Then, without saying a word, she extinguishes her candle and heads back towards Lourdes, paying no heed to the passionate interest of the throng. The apparition has been a long one, lasting a good three-quarters of an hour (from 7:15 to 8:00 A.M.).

However, there has been no miracle and no revelation. The crowd dwindles away, calm but perplexed. The police commissioner and the sergeant feel triumphant on two counts. First of all, the apparition has been a big disappointment. Secondly, the forces of law and order have done very well, avoiding any incident or accident. Those two facts, particularly the disappointment of the event, will be much discussed in the press in the days that follow.

That morning, however, a crowd of people gathers in front of The Jail. In a line that seems never to end, the

people want to see Bernadette in person, to touch or
embrace her. She herself protests: "And what will be next
after that?"

It is useless to resist. She tries to hold up the line by
delay but that does not work. Finally, to speed up the
process, she says: "Let them all in at once..." (H 5, p. 336).

To her surprise, her companion of the morning,
Jeanne Védère gets in the line and comes to present her
rosaries to Bernadette. She has three of them: her
ordinary rosary, that of the Seven Sorrows, and that of the
Camaldolese.

"You too!" exclaims Bernadette. "What in heaven's
name do you want me to do? I'm not a priest!"

With great difficulty the family manages to close the
door during the midday-meal hour, when there is a lull
in the crowd.

Bernadette takes advantage of this moment to carry
out her commission to Dean Peyramale. He is waiting for
her, hopefully and not without emotion.

"What did the lady say?"

"I asked her for her name...She smiled. I asked her
to make the rosebush flower, and she kept smiling. But
she still wants the chapel."

"Do you have the money to build this chapel?"

"No, Reverend Father."

"Neither do I. Tell the lady to give it to you."

Both he and Bernadette are disappointed that the
awaited answer was not given by the lady on this, the last
day.

Disguising herself as best she can, Bernadette heads
for 15 Rue du Bourg where Antoine Clarens lives. The
headmaster had invited her to take refuge from the crowd
in his own home. He is amazed to see her enter so
wholeheartedly into the play of his young children. His
youngest is Marie-Jeanne, age four.

But the crowd is gathering again outside The Jail.
They find out where she is hiding. The three medical
doctors who saw her early that morning have held a
meeting and are now demanding her return. Between

3:00 and 4:00 P.M. François Soubirous picks up his daughter and takes her back to The Jail. The line of people continues until the evening. Bernadette finally is worn out by all the embracing and begs for relief: "Lock the door!"

"The foul, somber hovel," mentioned in the prosecutor's report three days earlier has become a courtly waiting room. People want to meet Bernadette or leave money and gifts. Bernadette rejects their efforts with surprising vigor:

"That burns me," she exclaims, when they try to slip a gold coin into her hand.

That is lucky for her because traps have been laid by others. First a policeman was sent, because the officials assume that some sort of confidence game is involved. But that dodge was a bit too obvious. Then some private citizens were employed, including the wife of Sergeant D'Angla. Bernadette, however, does not know the technique of accepting tips suavely. She rejects all the money offered her with surprising vehemence.

Why is there such excitement and enthusiasm after the disappointment of the early morning? An event which took place on Bernadette's way from the grotto had served to rekindle people's hopes. On the slope leading up to the forest road, Bernadette had suddenly slowed down and almost come to a dead stop. Ganço, who was holding her with his right hand while fending off the crowd with his left, turned around. Bernadette was looking compassionately at a little girl wearing a red capulet. A native of Barèges, she had tried to approach Bernadette when she arrived at the grotto. Her name was Eugénie Troy and she was the same age as Bernadette. Obviously ill, she wore a bandage over her eyes because she could not tolerate light. Ganço noticed Bernadette's affectionate look.

"Let the girl from Barèges approach."

The crowd parted for her and the two young girls embraced each other, laughing and holding hands. Bernadette embraced her a second time and then

continued on her way, without having asked the girl her
name. Now the girl in the red capulet became the center
of everyone's attention because she had taken off her
bandage to look at the seer. The light of day, so painfully
dazzling for her, no longer bothered her at all. She was
carried away with joy.

"A miracle! A blind person has been healed!"

The news spread "with the rapidity of an electric
spark," to use the new metaphor of Dean Peyramale. The
crowd gathered around the girl from Barèges. She went
back down to the grotto and washed in the spring.
Excitement was at its peak and the crowd led her to
Prosecutor Dutour. They wanted this unbeliever to
corroborate the miracle, and they were scandalized by his
reserve and his skepticism.

Dean Peyramale seems more accepting, particularly
because of the warm feeling in the account of the girl's
father: "With the utmost conviction and with tears in his
eyes, he swears that his daughter recovered her sight
miraculously" (Letter of Peyramale, March 9, 1858; D 1,
pp. 230-231).

The people from Barèges testify in the same vein. On
the spot Peyramale formulates a verbal deposition for the
bishop, but with the reservation that there will be a closer
inquiry. The next day, March 5, he writes to the priest in
the girl's parish. There is a delay in that priest's response
because he is away. After the middle of March he does
come to Lourdes himself, and his report is as
disappointing as it possibly could be. The girl was never
blind, but the state of her health is not good. She is very
ill. Her joy over the visit to Lourdes had aroused illusions
shared by her parents. There can be no talk about a cure.
This verdict is confirmed by Doctor Theil, who is sent
there expressly to verify the situation. Peyramale's
disappointment is only deepened. The girl herself will die
the next year (June 9, 1859).

The Sick Boy on the Piqué Farm

Now Dean Peyramale is off on another track. People are
relating stories of a miracle in connection with
Bernadette's visits to the Piqué farm. A little sick boy
there had asked for her. Nine years old, he can neither
eat nor close his mouth. It remains wide open like an
oven. During Bernadette's visits he closes his mouth and
recovers his taste for life. The Dean and an assistant
curate go to the farm on March 15. "Noticeable
improvement," he notes on that day. But there must be a
much more "radical" cure before one can give a definite
answer on the matter or say, with St. Augustine, *"Causa
finita est."*
    Police pressure is exerted more emphatically on
Bernadette. She stops her visits to the farm, where the
mouth of the little boy has opened wide again.

Another Interrogation

On March 18 Bernadette submits to another formal
interrogation. She declares: "I do not believe that I have
cured anyone and, for that matter, I have done nothing to
that end. I do not know if I will go back to the grotto any
more" (H 5, p. 35).
    "She does not seem to want to tangle with the local
authorities," concludes the police commissioner.

The Real Problem

The real problem is no longer Bernadette herself so
much as it is the crowd that continues to frequent the
grotto. The candles multiply. There are 10 on March 18;
19 on March 21. On March 23 a plaster Virgin, furnished
by one Félix Maransin, is laid in the niche of the
apparition. At last one can point to an illicit place of

worship. There is a basis for legal action! Moreover, the people are drinking the water from the spring, which the pharmacist Pailhasson has declared to be "dangerous."

And yet the press has voiced a clear verdict. On the day after the "big day," the editorial in *Lavedan* is clearcut and straightforward:

> What disappointment!...How these poor credulous people have been humiliated...All the people who have realized, all too late unfortunately, the ridiculousness of their behavior and regretted their excessive credulity!

"The miracle is the amazing credulousness of this throng, who have not been undeceived even by the spectacle of their own disappointment," trumpets *Le Bagnérais*. Meanwhile *L'Ere impériale,* the official voice of the prefect, expresses regrets that the whole affair was not cut short by sending "the alleged saint of 11" (sic) "to the hospice as a sick person."

The strange affair overturns all customary habits and the best-laid plans.

Dean Peyramale.   Jacomet.

Bernadette in 1864.

Chapter 4

The Last Apparitions
March 25-July 16, 1858

In the wee hours of March 25, the feast of the
Annunciation, Bernadette is roused from her sleep by a
new "urge" to go to the grotto. Her parents want to stop
her but the urge is irresistible. Realizing it, her parents
make her wait. But at 5:00 A.M. she is on her way.

The Apparition of March 25

This time she has firmly decided to get some answer to
give to Dean Peyramale. After the rosary, *Aquerò*
approaches through the inner cavity. Bernadette,
overcome with joy, takes great pains to pose the question,
as formal and polite as a bow.

"Mademoiselle, would you be so kind as to tell me
who you are, if you please?"

Aquerò smiles. She does not reply. Bernadette
repeats the question insistently a second and third time.
Aquerò is still smiling all the while This time, however,
Bernadette will not let her get off because it is the
precondition laid down by the Dean for the building of a
chapel.

The fourth time Bernadette asks the question, *Aquerò*
stops "laughing." Her joined hands open out and extend
towards the ground. Then she joins them again around
her bosom, raises her eyes to the sky, and says:

Que soy era Immaculada Councepciou.

Immaculate Conception

Color comes back to Bernadette's face. She hastens
towards the rectory, continually repeating the words lest
she forget them as she did the words about the
procession. She avoids all questions and keeps repeating
to herself: *"Immaculada Coun...cet-tiou, Immaculada
Coun...cet-ciou."* She keeps stumbling over the final two
syllables. Finally she arrives at the rectory and fairly blurts
out to Dean Peyramale:

> *Que soy era Immaculada Councepciou.*

Peyramale staggers from shock. He is on the verge of
saying: "Vain little creature, you are the Immaculate
Conception!" But the words stick in his hoarse throat. He
realizes full well that Bernadette is not making that up
herself. He is fighting against a blinding light, and his
reason comes to aid his resistance. The Virgin was
conceived without sin, but she is not her conception.
Finally, his words come out: "A woman cannot have that
name! You are mistaken! Do you know what that means?"
Bernadette shakes her head: no.
"Then how can you say the words if you did not
understand them?"
"I kept repeating them along the way."
Peyramale feels all his anger slip‚ 'ng away. What
strange movement is shaking his chest? Is he sick? No, he
is holding in his sobs.
"She still wants the chapel," murmurs Bernadette in
the silent room.
The Dean mobilizes his last reserves of authority.
"Go back home. I will see you another day."
Bernadette is baffled. Why is the Dean angry? And
what do the words mean? She doesn't understand them at
all. She has never heard them before as such. But she
finds them very beautiful and gay. To be sure, the
expression *Immaculée Conception* had floated into her
ears in Church, on the feast day of December 8. But the

words were uttered in a foreign language, French, which
Bernadette did not know. And the concept itself is as
unknown to her as was the mystery of the Trinity. She
will learn the meaning of the term *Immaculada
Councepciou* only that evening, at the home of Estrade.
He is the first to even think of explaining it to her.

So, it was the Blessed Virgin then! At last Bernadette
can abandon herself to the joy that had invaded her that
morning.

But the title is upsetting. Peyramale has a fine time
formulating his theological objections in the letter he
writes to the bishop that evening. The believers are
annoyed by the unaccustomed expression. Each corrects
Bernadette in his or her own way, adapting the
expression to suit themselves. They have her say: "I am
the Virgin Immaculate." "I am Mary Immaculate." "I am
the Virgin of the Immaculate Conception."

Or strictly speaking: "Mary, the Immaculate
Conception."

They all reduce the disconcerting phrase to more
familiar models.

Once the letter is written and his duty to his bishop
done, Peyramale feels the weight of the whole thing
slipping off his shoulders. The child could not have made
that up. It can, it must have some meaning. He thinks of
the figures of speech he learned in the seminary. Thus
one says, "It is whiteness itself," instead of saying, "It is
very white." What is the name of that figure of speech?
And how might it apply to the dogma promulgated in
Rome four years earlier:

> We define that the Blessed Virgin was
> preserved from every taint of original
> sin...from the first moment of her
> conception.

Light suddenly begins to creep over the inner adhesion
which had been in his heart all the time, prior to any real
calculation.

Seventeenth Apparition / April 7, 1858

On Easter Tuesday, April 6, Bernadette again feels drawn
to the grotto. She enters the confessional after Vespers.
Antoinette Tardhivail, the assistant sacristan, sees her go
in and suspects something. She confides her guess to
some girl friends under the seal of secrecy. The word
spreads like a train of gunpowder.

Bernadette's friends are worried. The prosecutor had
interrogated her for four hours the previous week and
had forbidden her to return to the grotto (D 5, p. 75).
Before Vespers, however, Bernadette had journeyed to
the home of Blazy, the former mayor of Adé (four
kilometers from Lourdes). He had been healed at the
grotto and wanted to see her. Blazy's son offers to take
her during his break. It is a providential alibi.

The next morning, Easter Wednesday, Bernadette is
at the grotto before dawn. A few hundred people are
already there, and soon there will be a thousand.

Bernadette is already in ecstasy amid an impressive
air of silence. But there is some hubbub at the end of the
crowd, heavy footsteps, and an authoritative voice.
Someone is approaching the spot coveted by all.

"Let me through."

It is Doctor Dozous, who has wanted to examine the
ecstasy for some time. A fire lieutenant as well as medical
doctor, he has had one of his men, Martin Tarbès, alert
him. Dozous makes his way through the crowd amid
protests. Contrary to the respectful custom already
inaugurated at the grotto, he keeps his hat on. He moves
forward and faces the crowd with conviction.

"I do not come as an enemy but in the name of
science. I hurried here on the run" (for a moment he
uncovers his head, trickling with perspiration that glistens
in the glow of the candles) "and I cannot expose myself
to drafts of air. I am the only one who can verify the
religious event that is taking place here. Let me pursue
this study."

He sponges his head, annoyed that he may have

done the wrong thing by running. Suddenly a strange phenomenon attracts his attention and causes him to forget everything else. This particular day Bernadette has a long candle standing on the ground. It had been given to her by Blazy, her host of the previous day. To protect the flame from the wind, her two hands are on either side of the stem. She is holding the candle between her wrists. Her fingers are enveloping the lighted wick closely, like the two valves of a shellfish. Through the partly closed fingers one can see the flame licking her curved palms.

"She's burning!" cries someone in the crowd.

"Leave her alone," cries Dozous.

He does not believe his eyes. After the ecstasy is over, he examines the two hands of the seer. She has no idea of what is going on.

"Nou ya pas arré!" exclaims Dozous. "There's nothing wrong!" Faith has won in an instant. With the impetuous exuberance that is characteristic of him, Dozous proclaims the prodigious event to all in the *Café français,* to everyone in town, and to the police commissioner himself. The latter furtively noted down the doctor's excited remarks:

> For me it was a supernatural fact to see Bernadette on her knees before the grotto, in ecstasy, holding a lighted candle and covering the flame with her two hands, without her seeming to have the least impression of her hands' contact with the flame. I examined her hands. Not the slightest trace of burns.

A Time of Visionaries / April 13-July 11, 1858

After that date Bernadette withdraws into the shadows. She is threatened. The prefect wants to have done with this grotto. His plan is to have the seer hospitalized as a mentally ill patient. On May 4 he comes to Lourdes to preside over a review board. He declares forthrightly: "Any person who claims to see visions will be immediately arrested and brought to the hospital in Tarbes."

The very same day the police commissioner strips the grotto (an unauthorized place of worship!) of the religious objects with which it has been decorated. Bernadette's protective friends whisk her away. On March 8, without a word, she is sent to the waters of Cauterets to take care of her asthma. She quickly becomes the focal point of interest. Throughout the day people ask prayers from her. But the police commissioner of that town, who is in charge of surveillance over her, can only confirm her discretion and her refusal "of any and every sort of recompense" (D 2, p. 33).

In Lourdes itself, excitement grows. Bernadette's absence proves that she is not the cause. The problem is the confounded grotto! Believers regard the dismantling of May 4 as a sacrilege, and the spring attracts them. Pailhasson, the pharmacist, had opportunely declared the latter "dangerous." Now along comes Latour, the pharmacist from Trie, and finds in it "special curative properties which will rank it among those waters that constitute the mineral wealth of our province" (D 2, p. 34). This rave notice helps to nurture a dream of Mayor Lacadé: to erect a thermal spa. His reports allow the enticing project to leak out. Unfortunately serious laboratory analyses will show that the water of the grotto spring is quite ordinary, devoid of all the properties so earnestly envisioned by the municipality.

Pilgrimages by the people resist all efforts at dissuasion. They are organized spontaneously. There are prayers, hymns, candles, devotions, processions. The guilds of Lourdes have taken over management of the grotto. Right after the water appeared, Tarbès, the wheelwright, and Domengieux, the carpenter, dug a channel for it. On April 10, they fashioned a basin with clumps of turf. On April 24, Castérot, a tinsmith, installed

a zinc basin with three spigots. The carpenter then
fashioned a board with holes in it to hold the ever
increasing number of candles. And the quarrymen traced
out trails in the steep slope that descends to the grotto.

Sergeant D'Angla cannot get over it. These
people—usually "after gain"—give their time and money
for free. Gifts flow in to the grotto: gold and silver hearts,
statues, a gauze veil, and even a hunk of cheese. People
give everything they have. Money is deposited daily in the
cracks and crevices of the grotto. By whom? What for? No
one knows. Jacomet finds a gold piece there. What
substantial citizen left that gift? No substantial citizen at
all: a poor old woman in desperate need had given her
savings. "It's for the Virgin," she said.

"The richest offerings come from the poorer
people," notes the commissioner.

And the money is respected. It remains there without
anyone trying to profit from it. At one point Jacomet
thought he had uncovered an embezzlement scheme. On
March 1 the money had disappeared from the grotto.
However, investigation turned up nothing but a pious
initiative. Fourcade, the sacristan, had collected the money
and counted it. Then he had brought it to Dean
Peyramale to say a Mass on "the big day." The collecting
has gone on ever since then in regular and yet
spontaneous fashion.

Now, however, there are other phenomena of a
more debatable and disturbing cast. The praying had
started out with the accustomed forms, the rosary in
particular. But people's fervor, frustrated by the end of
the apparitions, now sometimes took on a feverish pitch.

On April 11, four days after the last public apparition
to Bernadette, five women got a ladder from the
Espélugues' farm. Fascinated by the mysterious caverns of
Massabielle, they raised the ladder on the right side of the
grotto at the back, the side opposite the spring. Seeing a
narrow crevice in the vault, the women climbed through
it with great difficulty and disappeared. All five of them

were carrying candles. A few minutes later they all
climbed back down, proclaiming that they had seen the
Virgin. They were church members of good reputation,
and Peyramale actually gave them a better reception than
he had given Bernadette.

On April 16, an expedition mounted by the police
commissioner would find the clue to this mystery. After
proceeding about ten meters in this rocky recess *(which
Bernadette was wholly unaware of),* today's cave
specialist will find the same thing that was found by the
alleged visionaries and the police: a white stalactite in the
form of a statue—but without a head. The play of shadow
and light and imagination supplied what was missing. The
solution of this puzzle does not stop the epidemic of
visionaries. In June, they multiply among the ranks of the
school children. By the beginning of July the count is up
to fifty or more (D 2, pp. 56-87).

The Grotto Off-limits

Officials do not wait until then to step in. On June 5, the
grotto is declared off-limits and barricaded. This
repression exasperates the population of Lourdes. The
barricades, erected on June 15, are demolished on June
17—by one of the people that the police commissioner
had requisitioned to erect them! Erected again on June
18, they are demolished on the night of June 27. They are
erected still again on June 28, demolished on the night of
July 4, and erected again on July 10.

Verbal reprimands rain down on visitors, as the
police take down names and addresses. People squeeze
through the disjointed boards. The pure prayer of the
apparitions period degenerates into pretence and
superstitious or feverish rites.

First Episcopal Intervention / July 11

Now the church authorities step in. On July 8, Dean
Peyramale alerts the bishop of Tarbes. On July 11, Bishop
Laurence, who had tried to keep his hopes up, denounces
the abuses. Much to everyone's astonishment, they
disappear in the twinkling of an eye. There will be no
more problems with visionaries at the grotto.

The Final Meeting / July 16, 1858

Bernadette, now forgotten, had stayed completely out of
this feverish business. She respected the order
promulgated and counseled people against crossing the
barricades.

Five days after the episcopal intervention that had
restored peace and quiet, it is the feast of Our Lady of
Mount Carmel. Bernadette suddenly feels drawn to
Massabielle. Caught once again between the claims of
obedience and the invincible attraction of the grotto,
Bernadette compromises a bit. She waits until the
evening. Then, camouflaged in a dark-colored hood that
she had borrowed, she hastens through the twilight. But
instead of going towards the Pont Vieux, which leads
down to Massabielle she takes the opposite direction. She
stays on the right bank and enters the Ribère meadow.
Groups of people are there on their knees, praying
silently in the direction of the barricaded grotto across
the way. Bernadette kneels down, too, and lights her
candle. It is one flame among many in the gathering
darkness. She has come alone with her Aunt Lucile. Two
other parishioners join them silently.

The rosary is scarcely begun when Bernadette's
hands open wide in a greeting of joyous surprise. Her

face pales and lights up, as it had during the fifteen days of apparitions. She recites the rosary for some length of time that no one thought to measure. Then she gets up. It is over. This final apparition had been a silent one, like the first few. On the way back home Bernadette had only this to say:

> I saw neither the boards nor the Gave. It seemed to me that I was in the grotto, no more distant than the other times. I saw only the Holy Virgin.

It was the last time she would see her on this earth.

Louise Castérot Soubirous, Bernadette's mother.

Chapter 5

Witness on All Fronts
1858-1860

During the apparitions, Bernadette in ecstasy had been a witness without realizing it. The transfiguration of her face and the transport of her prayer had shaken and converted many onlookers, though Bernadette did not notice this (H 3, pp. 30-135).

During those moments Bernadette did not have to defend herself against questioners. She had not even heard those who might by chance try to communicate with her. She was cut off from the outside world.

When an apparition was over, however, the questions poured in from all sides. All the inquisitive questions and hypotheses, be they sober minded or outlandish, were directed to her. In the course of the day she became the prey of questioners, both believers and unbelievers, admirers and adversaries. From February 21 on, she undergoes regular interrogations and cross-examinations by police officials, magistrates, doctors commissioned by the prefect to declare her mentally ill, and priests. The latter she fears the most, even as she fears God himself. Because she alone can tell people anything about the apparition and its message, this frail child becomes the caryatid on which rests the future of the pilgrimage, the chapel that is to be built, and everything else.

How did Bernadette get through it all without losing her calmness, her equilibrium, or her mind? Herein lies one of the astonishing aspects of the whole Bernadette phenomenon. She answers people without calculation or formulations, without fear or complacence She speaks in the briefest and most direct terms, unwittingly carrying out the Gospel maxim: "When they bring you before synagogues, rulers and authorities, do not worry about

View of Lourdes

The Soubirous home. (From a Spanish engraving.)

how to defend yourselves or what to say. The Holy Spirit
will teach you at that moment all that should be said"
(Lk 12:11-12).

Therein lay Bernadette's whole secret. That is how
the little David withstood the Goliaths of Church and
State. And those who did not surrender to her
acknowledged at least her intelligence and her sincerity.

Of course she had supporters who helped her to
extricate herself from difficulty in all the maneuvers
designed to demean her or show her up. Mr. Dufo, a
lawyer who was an ardent believer in the apparitions,
began to warn her of certain traps about midway during
the fifteen days of apparitions. Judge Pougat, the President
of the Tribunal, did so from a very different motive. Lost
in the judiciary, into which he was propelled by political
supporters, he warned Bernadette about illegal or
irregular summonses from the imperial prosecutor, his
subordinate. Dutour was aware of these warnings, but he
did not know how to go about denouncing his superior.
The notes that he scratched out on the subject bear
witness to his embarrassment. But he is not so
embarrassed to reproach the seer herself: 'Beware,
Bernadette. There is a certain gentleman near the portal
who is giving you advice. He will not stop you from going
to prison!"

Half in French and half in *patois,* Bernadette quickly
responded: *"Que deouét parla debout àou même
Moussu, "*: "You should speak directly to that gentleman."

Her candor accomplished more than the advice she
received. What was true of her ecstasy was also true of
her testimony: her secret lay in nothing else but her
transparency.

First Communion

Bernadette is now going to school. It offers her
protection against intrusive people. On June 3 she makes
the First Communion which she had so greatly desired.

During the retreat before First Communion, Dean
Peyramale had authorized a strange woman to approach
Bernadette and ask her a question: "Reverend Father
forbids you to go to the grotto. What if the Virgin were to
order you to go there, what would you do?"

"I would go back and ask Reverend Father for
permission" (Letter of Peyramale: D 2, no. 314, p. 359).

The day after her Communion, Emmanuélite Estrade
asks her another question: "What made you happier: First
Communion or the apparitions?"

Her reply was simple and direct: "The two things go
together, but they cannot be compared. I was very happy
with both" (A. Barbet, PONev 925).

Cure Seekers and Curiosity Seekers

The summer brings to Lourdes, the crossroads of the
roads and valleys in the spa region, the usual file of
vacationing tourists, starting with the Emperor. The
Parisian press has written about apparitions. The rumor is
sustained in pious bulletins, particularly in *Le Rosier de
Marie*. The cure seekers and the curious flock to
Bernadette. She is the only recourse for those who want
to find out something and form a judgment.

In The Jail, life is disorganized by perpetual visits.
Every day the Soubirous resist people's efforts, one more
ingenious than the next, to leave some offering.
Bernadette is adamant, not without flashes of temper. One
day some wealthy visitors ask her little brother to go for
some water in the grotto. On his return he is given a gold
piece for his trip. When he gets back to The Jail, very
proud of the money he has earned, he gets a royal box
on the ear from his sister. He must go and give back the
money at once. He himself recounted this incident.

In July Charles Madon, a young lawyer of 32 from
Beaune, noted down his conversation with Bernadette on
the spot. He is won over immediately by her
physiognomy. She is "intelligent, gracious, and

modest—a pleasure to look at." But her asthma disturbs
him. She coughs frequently. He asks her some questions.
"Have you prayed for your own cure?"
"No."
"And your secrets? What are they about?"
"They concern only me."
"If the pope were to ask you for them, would you
tell them to him?"
"No."
"What if your confessor refused to let you receive
Communion during Eastertide because of your refusal?"
"No."
"I know one of your secrets. It is that you will be a
nun."
Bernadette laughs: "It's not that. They are more
serious."
"Does it bother you that people ask for your
secrets?"
"No, but the apparition told me not to tell them."
Through able questioning, however, the visitor did
manage to find out some things about the secrets. They
were spoken "in patois...on several different days." They
concern only "her own life." On other occasions she will
say that they do not concern the pilgimage, or France, or
the world. That is what justifies her discretion.
On July 17, Bishop Thibault of Montpellier lands in
Lourdes. He asks to see Bernadette and Dean Peyramale
eagerly summons her to the rectory. Her poverty and
simplicity make a deep impression on the bishop. He
would like her to take a little offering from him. No,
thank you. Then what about this beautiful rosary that was
indulgenced by Pope Pius IX himself? No, thank you. If
she doesn't want a gift, then how about trading her rosary
for this one?
"No, Reverend Father, I prefer my own rosary."
Throughout the conversation Bernadette addresses
the visitor as Reverend Father. She does not know he is a
bishop any more than she knew what the mystery of the
Trinity was two months earlier. The whole atmosphere

and pageant of this meeting is far less impressive to her than was her visit to the Tarbes seminary. Then she ran to the window of the parlor and looked out in astonishment at all the men in cassocks: "Oh! Oh!"

On July 20, Bishop Cardon de Garsignies of Soissons asks for her. He questions her about heaven. Didn't she have that experience? Her reply is simply: "I know nothing, Monseigneur. I am ignorant."

Like his colleague from Montpellier, he leaves Lourdes disturbed, challenged, bolstered in his inner convictions, and finally, convinced.

The two bishops hasten to tell what they know to Bishop Laurence of Tarbes. They urge him to get involved. And so, on July 28, at 11:00 A.M., he signs a formal document establishing a commission of inquiry.

On the same day the wife of Admiral Bruat, governess of the imperial prince, comes to Lourdes with her children, a priest and a nun. They have a conversation with Bernadette.

"Since the Virgin was married to Saint Joseph, she ought to have a ring, shouldn't she?" asks the priest.

"No, Father, she didn't have any."

The Sister asks Bernadette to take them to the grotto, but she refuses.

"No! No! I am forbidden."

It is not hard for the party to find a guide because the believers are on holiday. Just for spite, some of them have given the alert to Callet, the rural constable, who is supposed to accost violators of the ordinance and take down their names and addresses for the police blotter. The believers would like to see Callet get into a real jam by accosting such an important personage. Awakened from his after-lunch nap, Callet arrives at the grotto and sees the women praying despite the "no entrance" signs. He suddenly senses the trap, as a private might who is just about to hit a general in civvies. Amiably he notes down the identity of the visitor in his own inimitable spelling: "Amral Bruhat's widow, govorniss of the children of France and her family in the company of a sistir."

To save face and reputation, he climbs over the rock
and drops down inside the barricaded grotto in order to
throw the bouquets left there into the Gave. It is one of
his duties every day: a sad duty but at least it gives him an
alibi. The Admiral's wife is a great lady and she notices
his confusion.

"Guard, Sir, would you be so kind as to fill this
decanter with water from the spring for me?"

He does it quite readily, also giving her the clods of
earth and the few stones she asks for. He refuses the
100-sou coin that the Sister wants to give him. That
evening the Admiral's widow arranges to have the money
placed in his home while he is out, so that he cannot
refuse it.

While she is still in prayer at the grotto, Louis
Veuillot, editor of L'Univers, arrives in a white hat. Callet
takes down his name too, as Veuillot exclaims: "And so
they want to stop people from praying to the good God
here!" (D 3, p. 46).

He goes back to Lourdes and arranges a meeting
with Bernadette at the place of Pailhasson, the pharmacist
and chocolate seller. He conducts a regular interview
before a large audience. Father Pomian translates for him.
He keeps insisting on the secrets though Bernadette
resists and Father Pomian keeps trying to dissuade him:
"That's not important." Veuillot is very moved. After
Bernadette leaves, he writes: "She is illiterate,, but she is
worth more than I" (D 3, p. 47).

A month later in Paris, on August 28, the interview
will fill five columns on page one of L'Univers.

On July 30, Father Hyacinthe Loison subjects
Bernadette to a regular cross-examination. Then a famous
preacher, he will renounce his vows later on.

During the same time period Father Nègre, a pious
Jesuit, employs all the tools of his theology to prove to
Bernadette that she "saw the devil."

"Et diáble n'ey pas aoutá beróy qu'éro," replies
Bernadette: "The devil is not as beautiful as she."

According to the demonology of the visitor, Satan is

facile in undergoing metamorphosis but is unable to
pretty up all his attributes. He has bestial characteristics
and hides them.
"You did not see the feet. Her feet were hidden."
"Yes, I did. She had bare feet, very pretty."
"You didn't see the hands! They were hidden in the
shadows, weren't they?"
"No, I saw them and they were very nice" (A VII, p. 264).
At this point Bernadette breaks off the interview with
this remark to Antoinette Tardhivail: *"N'at bo créde,
tournéns-en":* "He doesn't wish to believe. Let's get out of here."
The dialogue in this conversation, reported by
Antoinette, might seem highly improbable. Twenty years
later, however, Father Nègre unwittingly acknowledged
that that had indeed been his idea and his line of thought.
Replying to Father Cros in a letter dated September 18,
1878, he writes:

> I know (sic) that in his appearances the
> Devil ordinarily takes the feet of some
> beast.
>   Since the Incarnation...God does not
> deign to permit the Devil to take the full
> and perfect form of humanity. He must
> betray himself by some bestial
> characteristic (A VI).

Other interrogators threaten Bernadette with hell fire
(D 5, p. 292), drag her to perilous theological heights, or
try to trap her in the inextricable toils of casuistry. She
replies clearly and briefly—right to the point, as did Joan
of Arc. The following dialogue takes place between
Bernadette and a missionary in the Tarbes diocese:
"Since the Holy Virgin promised you heaven, you
need not worry about taking care of your soul."
"Oh, Reverend Father! I will go to heaven if I do as
one ought."
"But what do you mean by 'doing as one ought'?"
"Oh! I don't have to tell someone like you that,
Reverend Father!"

Others will ask her to do impossible things, such as duplicating the smile of the Virgin.

Bernadette is under a severe handicap in giving her testimony. Until the beginning of that year she had only spoken the dialect of her valley. French is a foreign language to her, and so there are misunderstandings and errors. Realizing this, Bernadette makes an effort to speak French from July on. She speaks "a very incorrect French," notes Balech de Lagarde, when he comes to interview the new celebrity for *Courrier français* on September 24. The journalist earns his pay and questions Bernadette about everything: "The country is talking about you a great deal...Does that please you?"

"It doesn't matter to me."

"Several journals have printed your name. Have you been told this?"

"Yes."

"Have you seen the journals?"

"No, I can scarcely read at all."

"Do you like that?"

"Oh, not at all, no!"

Then the journalist tried to "dazzle" her, to use his own expression: "Listen, Bernadette, you must come to Paris with me. In three weeks you will be rich...I will take care of your good fortune."

"Oh, no, no! I want to remain poor."

His urgings are in vain.

On October 5, 1858, the vacationing Emperor, now under stress from the Lourdes affair, orders the barricades removed from the grotto. The measure earns him great popularity.

Facing the Episcopal Commission

The commission of inquiry appointed by the bishop sets to work. On November 17, Bernadette is subjected to her first ecclesiastical interrogation. She displays the same limpid assurance before the four canons. She unhesitatingly distinguishes between what she knows and what she has forgotten: dates, for example. The message itself, however, is very much present to her. On only one point is her memory a blank: the famous procession requested by the apparition on March 2. Her recollection of it disintegrated under the ire of Dean Peyramale. She can only say: "I am not sure that this order was given to me; but in regard to the construction of the chapel, I have always been sure and I am still certain now" (B 1, p. 194).

In mid-September the Soubirous family leaves The Jail for a more wholesome room in Deluc's place. He runs a pastry and coffee shop, and he is vaguely related to the Soubirous through the Castérot family. So the family has now heeded the warning given by the three doctors who came and hurriedly examined Bernadette on Thursday, March 4: "If you want to preserve your children, you must not remain here" (H 5, p. 354, note 280).

The Gras Mill / 1859

During the first quarter of 1859, the Gras mill is vacant and François Soubirous again tries his luck there. It is there that a young English tourist, R.S. Standen, meets Bernadette on April 19. François has regained his craft and his dignity. He seems quite "respectable," notes the visitor. And Bernadette is a "pretty looking girl." She speaks "very intelligently" in explaining the functioning of the mill, familiar to her from early childhood. It is good for her to find herself out in the open air again, along a brook. Her asthma is much better.

The young man is particularly struck by the fact that Bernadette is completely unconcerned about the miracles which the whole town is talking about. The English youth mentions a few to her. Bernadette, totally put off, rejects them all with one outburst: "There's no truth in all that" (D 5, p. 51, note 124).

Between August 8 and August 12, an overworked Bernadette is suffering from another bout of asthma.

Dominique Mariote and Paul de Lajudie find her confined
to bed. They take advantage of the opportunity to
question her at length. Each of the two men makes his
own separate notes of the interview (B 1, pp. 202-210).

"Why were you forbidden to go to the grotto?"

"Because everyone was following me."

"Why is it that you no longer go there now?"

"Oh, back then, I was really pushed to go!" (Said
with great emphasis, notes Mariote here.)

"You were really pushed?"

"Yes, I was really pushed!"

"But who was pushing you?"

"I don't know, but I was being pushed and I could
not stay away."

"And now you are no longer pushed?"

"No, Father."

"Have you seen the Holy Virgin since then?"

"No, Father, I haven't seen her."

"Not even on the day of your First Communion?"

"No, Father."

"When did you make your First Communion?"

"Last year."

"And when you go to the grotto, you do not see her
any more?"

"No, Father."

They question her at length on the secrets, but to no
avail. When she bids them goodbye, it is with a natural
and amiable smile (D 5, pp. 318-319; B 1, p. 211).

One of the two, Paul de Lajudie, returns to question her
on September 28: "Would you tell your secret to the Pope?"

"The Holy Virgin forbade me to tell it to any
person...The Pope is a person."

"But the Pope has the power of Jesus Christ."

"Yes, the Pope is very powerful on earth, but the
Holy Virgin is powerful in heaven."

He, too, notes Bernadette's complete indifference to
the miracles.

"To your knowledge, have there been miraculous
events, cures worked miraculously?"

"I have been told that there have been miracles; but to my knowledge, no!"

He expresses his astonishment. Bernadette becomes more explicit.

"Not to my personal knowledge. I have not seen them."

"People say that you have contributed to some of these miracles. Is that true?"

Smiling, she replies: "Oh no, Sir, not a one!"

To help her asthma and to give her refuge from such importunities, Bernadette is sent to the waters of Cauterets again this year.

A Life on Four Fronts

During this period Bernadette is living a life on four fronts:

1. She is working to earn bread for her family, spending whole days as a "little nursemaid" at the home of Armantine Grenier (D 6, p. 74, note 180).

2. She is helping out at home and playing her role as the eldest child, particularly vis-a-vis that madcap Toinette.

3. Prevented from attending school regularly, she is trying to make up for being behind with the help of kind lessons from Antoinette Tardhivail.

4. Finally, she is answering questions for all sorts of visitors, whether she meets them at her home or is summoned elsewhere to see them: e.g., the rectory, the hospice, the *Hôtel des Pyrénées,* and private homes. Her testimony is a deciding factor in the establishment of the pilgrimage while the episcopal commission is at its work.

"Available to everyone, she edified some and astounded or disconcerted others," notes Dean Peyramale

in his letter of May 17, 1860 (D 6, p. 110). As Father
Pomian puts it, she herself is "the best proof of the
apparition" (PANev 1142). But at what a price!

It is not only her gift for repartee but also the natural
economy of her responses that saves her. She responds
directly to the question asked her, never going further.
She is completely indifferent to the effect she produces.
She makes no effort to convince people, avoiding debate
and discouraging lengthy discussion. She knows how to
unwind naturally, and this spares her much useless
fatigue.

The aptness of her remarks and her behavior
astonishes all those who know her. Some of them have
noted that she never displayed so much intelligence as
she did in giving her testimony. This charisma, evident
most fully when Bernadette faces the authorities (see Lk
12:11), is also present when she meets visitors of all sorts
during the course of an ordinary day. It enables her to
avoid enormous risks.

But it is an impossible life for the Soubirous. At the
mill their natural generosity is dangerously gaining the
upper hand again. They are too receptive, too
accommodating, both to their customers and to the
visitors from whom they will accept nothing. Louise again
begins to offer people a collation, and to say to customers
in a tight fix; "You will pay when you can."

The hospice school in Lourdes,
where Bernadette lived after the apparitions.

Chapter 6

Bernadette under Protection

Dominiquette Concerned

At the beginning of 1860, Dominiquette Cazenave is concerned about this "confusion." She seeks out Dean Peyramale: "You are not going to leave her in the world!" (A VII, p. 73).

Dean Peyramale had been thinking about the matter. As early as the summer of 1858, he has suggested to Bernadette that he might be able to let her live with the Sisters who ran the hospice. But she had replied: "Oh, I understand exactly what you mean, Reverend Father; but I love my mother and father so much!" (D 3, p. 326).

Now the project begins to take definite shape. Mayor Lacadé, who subsidizes the hospice, figures out a special status for Bernadette. She can be taken in as a sick person who is indigent (D VI, p. 77). But under the cover of this administrative formula, arrangements will be made so that she can pursue her studies at the hospice school.

Her parents are averse to the idea of separating from Bernadette, just as she is averse to parting from them. They are promised that their daughter will come to see them "freely," but in the company of a nun (BARBET, pp. 129-30; D 6, p. 77).

With the Sisters

On Sunday, July 15, Bernadette is installed in the hospice, where she will stay until she leaves Lourdes. Now she is protected at last, a step that was necessary in one sense but also unfortunate in another sense. For her testimony now loses something of its vivacity and freedom. She can no longer deftly deal with people as she once did in her own natural way. Now she is living under the watchful

eye of the nuns and the more distant surveillance of Dean
Peyramale. She is the seer who is led into the parlor and
presented to visitors in humiliating terms. For the
pedagogy of that day insisted on repressing pride in every
circumstance that might prompt one to indulge in it. Thus
Bernadette is submitted to alternating doses of admiration
and humiliation that would have shattered a less solid
character.

Her keen lack of self-interest also loses its edge. In
Bernadette's absence the family will be less scrupulous on
this point. Thus in October 1860, after Bernadette has left
home, Azun de Bernétas finally manages to get Louise to
accept money to defray expenses for her trips to the
grotto on his behalf. He had asked her to make a novena
there for him. It was, of course, fair compensation for the
time she spent doing this, when she might have been
earning money for food; and it had taken a great deal of
persuasion on his part. But the fact remains that such
remuneration would have been out of the question if
Bernadette had still been living at home.

She herself no longer has the right to refuse
"dishonest money." She must accept it for work, and that
costs her more than anything else. But in that area as in
everything else, she was trained to obedience and to fight
against her own instincts. She never really was permitted
to decide for herself.

Finally Bernadette quits her own milieu because
there are no longer any boarders in the poor children's
class that she had been attending. She must now choose
between the "first class" composed of middle-class girls
and the "second class" attended by less affluent but decent
girls. On her own request she is put into the latter class.

The advantage for her is that now, for the first time
in her life, she is going to attend a regular year of school.
It is not easy for her, because she is now sixteen years
old and is not used to this kind of effort. She sometimes
despairs when she finds that the things she has so
painstakingly memorized quickly vanish from her mind:
"You would have to cram the book into my head!"

She is more at ease with needlework. The intelligence and expertise of her hands proves to be exceptional, especially in embroidery.

"At recreation she is the life of the party. Always gay, she breathes life into the play of the younger classes, though she quickly gets out of breath' (testimony of Sister Philomène Camès, B 1, p. 239).

Bernadette's "Faults"

Seeing her day after day, the nuns learn to recognize her "faults." She knows what she wants. Her bouts of stubbornness astonish them. One day she holds out against Sister Victoire Poux, who wants her to change her Sunday dress (for no good reason). When they refuse to let her go home to her family, she protests: "You promised me."

But at least she protests only in private, never "in the presence of the children" (A VII, p. 191, no. 136). Sensitive to little injustices, she is quick to defend others against mistakes made by those in charge. That is viewed as a weakness, and her prankishness is not at all appreciated as proper to a "seer."

The latter trait posed the greatest obstacle to her canonization later on. The most serious incident occurred in the early summer of 1861. Bernadette was on the first floor of the hospice with Julie Garros (age 10), a very lively little girl. She was Bernadette's tutor for lessons, though she was the younger one. The window looked out on the kitchen garden, where the two girls noticed some enticing strawberries. They were formally forbidden to go into that garden, but no one had ever said specifically that they could not collect strawberries. Bernadette has an idea: "I will throw my shoe out the window. You go get it and bring back some strawberries" (D 6, p. 81).

During the beatification process for Bernadette, the devil's advocate stressed the gravity of this incident. Speaking in Latin, he noted that this was "undoubtedly *malitia* and a patent violation of discipline." *Malitia* means a deliberate inclination to do evil. Fortunately for Bernadette, it was a sin of youth that she would redeem with her later life.

Sister Victorine was astonished to see that Bernadette entertained fancies about her dress and was concerned with beauty care. One day she found her trying to "widen her skirt" after the pattern of the crinolines that Dean Peyramale and the clergy were calling "diabolic." Another time Bernadette was caught trying to add a piece of wood to her corset as a stay (D 6, p. 82, note 212).

Bernadette was 17 at the time, and the stirrings of nature were not foreign to her. In those days such behavior posed a problem. Today the absence of such behavior would be more disturbing.

On the other hand all recognized her respect for God, the seriousness of her prayer, and her exacting demands on herself and her sisters. But on one occasion Sister Victorine got a very bad impression when she heard Bernadette telling her sister Toinette the following: "Don't learn to read."

Bernadette was speaking to her near a window in the corridor of the hospice. Sister Victorine, who just happened to catch the conversation in passing, was astonished by this bad advice and spoke to Bernadette.

"Ah, we are from a family where that is worth more," was Bernadette's reply.

What Bernadette feared for her sister was the bad example of other young ladies, who hid cheap novels in their missal and read them on the sly (B 1, 242). But Bernadette wouldn't tattle on them for all the money in the world.

The hardest thing to repress in her is her repugnance towards money. At first she would "let it fall on the ground." Now she says, in a scarcely encouraging tone: "There is a poor-box."

And if, despite all her efforts, the money ends up in her hands, she hurriedly makes sure that it will be passed into the hands of the Mother Superior.

She is attached to nothing and readily gives away what she has (D 6, p. 84). Gifts and personal objects do not accumulate in her little wardrobe. Nothing special or peculiar can be found in it, except the flask of wine that astounded Sister Victorine. Her parents bring her some wine now and then "to fortify her," according to the accepted local formula.

If Bernadette takes snuff, it is because Doctor Balencie has prescribed it for her asthma. But it is the cause of incidents. One day during class she offers a pinch to her neighbors. Their cascade of sneezes provokes the year's wildest fit of laughing.

Bernadette brings gaiety wherever she goes. Indeed she brings just a bit too much, according to the opinion current in her day. At recreation she flees from all serious subjects, even right after meetings of the Children of Mary. She prefers play and good fun. She takes more delight in giving pleasure to others than to herself, except when her companions ask her to give an account of the apparitions.

"Oh, please leave me be," she implores, "I must tell it to so many strangers" (PATarb 283, D 7, p. 29).

Some Acknowledged Good Qualities

She is closely watched to protect her from the curious. Her piety is ordinary but irreproachable. She always makes her Sign of the Cross as she did "during the apparitions," even when she is alone. This action is very edifying. She is officially permitted to go to Communion every Sunday and even now and then during the week. In that particular era, such frequent Communion is a privilege (D 6, p. 83, notes 216-217).

People also respect her scrupulousness about not taking a throat lozenge the evening before she is to receive Communion, even if she has a cough. She does not want to risk breaking her fast. On that point she is only observing the ordinary teaching of the time.

But Bernadette has no talent for prayer, as she readily admits: "Oh dear! I do not know how to meditate."
"She buckled down to it in the long run," adds Sister Victorine (A VII, p. 191, no. 136; RSL, no. 15, p. 106).

The Worst Trial

Around the end of 1861, Bernadette is photographed for the first time. Father Bernardou, professor of chemistry in the minor seminary, obtains Dean Peyramale's permission to take her picture.

Like a demanding movie director, he insists that Bernadette adopt exactly the same pose and expression that she had during the apparitions. Bernadette protests vigorously: "But she isn't here!"

Father Bernardou will hear no such talk. He is fully taken up with his project.

Did those involved permit him to preserve her image because they were afraid of losing it altogether? Periodic crises with her asthma raise fears about how long she is going to live. She cannot breathe, and the air accumulated in her lungs chokes her. She flushes and turns purple. The first time this happened, her parents were summoned during the night (testimony of Jean-Marie Soubirous, PONev, 164v; D 7, p. 112, note 623).

Was that her worst trial? No, according to her own words during one such crisis: "I prefer that to receiving visits" (D 7, p. 112).

Visitors come by the hundreds, then by the thousands. It becomes intolerable, to the point of nausea. Bernadette is very reluctant to meet visitors, especially when they interrupt her recreation. Sister Victorine tells us about it:

I saw her begin to cry in the doorway,
when there were 20 or 30 or 40 people in
the drawing room waiting for her...These
big tears would come. I would say to her:
Courage!

Bernadette would wipe away her tears, enter the room, greet everyone graciously, and then answer their questions (A VII, p. 197, no. 167; RSL. no. 15, p. 108). Then she would return to her play as if nothing had happened (PATarb, p. 229, no. 49).

The most painful thing for her was to be treated as a saint, though she herself did nothing to encourage such treatment. People would ask her to touch holy objects.

"I am forbidden to do that."

Then people would resort to subterfuges. Even distinguished visitors would drop their rosary so that she might pick it up for them. Her clear-headedness and keenness would neutralize her sense of obligation. One day she said: "I'm not the one who dropped it."

Another time, Sister Victorine tells us, several women approached her from behind: "If I could only cut off a bit of her dress!"

"What imbeciles you are!" said the seer (A VII, p. 197).

Now that Bernadette knows how to write, the forced labor of writing documents in her own hand or signing them is added to her other duties. She begins her new job on January 1, 1859 when she is ordered to write several copies of model prayers and aspirations, none of which she understands. She soon finds her own master formula: p.p. Bernadette. This abbreviated autograph, which she wrote on hundreds of pictures, means: "Pray for Bernadette."

People often present her their rosaries to bless. "I do not wear a stole," she tells them. And she is asked about her secrets day after day: "If you cannot tell them, it is a useless revelation," argue three Jesuits.

"It is useful for me," she replies.

"Why have you hidden them from your confessor?" asks Father Cabane.

"They are no sin," replies Bernadette.

The Final Episcopal Interrogation

On December 7, 1860, Bernadette is summoned for a solemn and final interrogation before Bishop Laurence in the Tarbes chancery. The bishop's face is a smooth, imperturbable mask. He is surrounded by the sharply chiselled faces of the twelve members of the commission. The Secretary, Fourcade, tirelessly keeps on filling up the big sheets of white paper in front of him.

"Did the Holy Virgin have a halo?" asks one of the commission members.

"A halo?"

Bernadette is not familiar with the word. When it is explained to her, she quickly replies: "She was enveloped with a soft light."

"Did you get a good look at it?"

"Oh, yes."

"And did this light appear at the same time as the apparition?"

"It came before it and remained a little after it."

"The idea of making you eat some kind of grass doesn't seem to me to be an idea worthy of the Holy Virgin," remarks another member of the commission.

"Well, we eat salad all right," replies Bernadette.

At the end of the interview she is asked to show exactly how the Virgin spoke the words of March 25: "I am the Immaculate Conception." Bernadette gets up, stretches out her arms, and joins her hands. Something happens as they watch the enactment of this inspired gesture:

> Two tears are seen running down the face of the old bishop. After the meeting, still deeply moved, he says to a vicar-general: "Did you see that child?" (SEMPÉ, p. 201).

Thirteen months later, on January 18, 1862, the bishop issues his official letter recognizing the apparitions:

We judge that the Immaculate Mother of
God truly appeared to Bernadette.

The judgment is solidly grounded on the spiritual
fruits of the pilgrimage, the cures, and Bernadette herself.

Bernadette and Her Doctor

Shortly afterwards, people again have reason to fear they
are going to lose her. On April 28, 1862, she receives the
sacrament of Extreme Unction. She does indeed seem to
be *in extremis*, breathing her last. She cannot take
communion the regular way. She manages to get a little
morsel of the host down her throat with help from a little
water from the grotto.

Is it the end? No. The face of the dying girl changes.
Her blocked breathing becomes more easy. Relieved, she
smiles. She would like to eat, to get up out of bed.
Mother Superior says no. There will be time enough for
that tomorrow.

The next day, April 29, Doctor Balencie is rather
surprised to find her in the parlor. He hides his
astonishment: "Well, well! The medicines we have
prescribed have done their work!"

"But I didn't take them," observes Bernadette (D 6,
p. 360, no. 1300).

In town, where reports of Bernadette's death agony
have heightened emotions, there is now talk of a miracle.
But it is one of those sudden remissions common in
cases of asthma. There is no mysticism whatsoever in
Bernadette's own conclusion:

If I am sick again, I will beg the doctor to pay close
attention...He took my illness for another,
and I could have died (D 6, pp. 360-61).

The formal judgment of the bishop of Tarbes silences
those who are hostile to Bernadette. But now even more
subtle questions are formulated sometimes: "Suppose the

bishop of Tarbes had judged that you were deluded, what would you have replied?" asks Father Corbin.

"I could never say that I did not see or hear what I did see and hear," replies Bernadette.

The year 1862 brings her an occasion of great joy. At the end of August she meets her godfather, Jean-Marie Védère, who is home on leave from the service. He had won the Legion of Honor medal in 1859 for his actions in the battle of Solferino. Bernadette meets him for the first and last time, bathed in the glory of his legendary deeds and his remoteness.

The year 1863 goes on in the monotonous rhythm of boarding-school life and enforced visits. In June of that year Bernadette meets a visitor who really moves her. It is Father Alix. The famous and rather worldly orator had undergone the shock of a thorough conversion at Lourdes. He confides the story to Bernadette. She recognizes her own experience in what he tells her. Twice she exclaims: "It's the Blessed Virgin, Father, the Blessed Virgin, who did that" (D 7, p. 244, no. 1457).

In October 1863, her picture is taken for the second time, thanks to the tactful approach of an itinerant photographer, Billard-Perrin of Pau.

Photos of Bernadette by Billard-Perrin (October 1863).

Chapter 7

The Shepherdess and the Sculptor

1863-1864

Now Bernadette is requisitioned for a delicate matter. The Lacour ladies from Lyon are devoted adherents of Lourdes, and they have had a chalet built for them on what is now the esplanade. They decide to replace the little statue, which the people of Lourdes have placed in the grotto, with a statue to be hewn out of Carrara marble. It will depict the apparition life-size, and it is to be "as exact as possible."

With the consent of the bishop of Lourdes they sign a contract with the sculptor, Joseph Fabisch, a member of the Lyon Academy of Sciences, Belles-Lettres and Arts. It is a fabulous contract for 7,000 *francs-or,* plus his expenses. He is to begin with a trip to Lourdes to question Bernadette. Fabisch is a specialist on this particular subject, for it is he who did the spire-statue for Notre Dame de Fourvière and the one of Notre Dame de la Salette.

First Meeting

On September 17, 1863 he arrives in Lourdes. Bernadette is summoned from recreation to meet him. The sculptor notes her features with an expert's eye:

> Her figure, while not possessing the regularity sought by the sculptor, has something very *simpatico* about it: a charm that commands respect and inspires faith (Memorandum of October 27, 1878, p. 3).

He is sympathetic, but he is also a bit on edge and out of sorts. In doing the La Salette statue, he had

Our Lady of Lourdes. This statue, showing Mary as she appeared in the apparitions, was formally inaugurated on April 4, 1864.

negotiated for permission to interpret the "eccentric"
pieces of information given by those who had seen the
Virgin. In this case, however, the contract obliges him to
conform to the information given by the seer. But might
they not be contrary to the "rules of art," which he
believes to be the last court of appeal? He prepared
twenty questions in pencil on a piece of notepaper, which
is extant today, and he recorded Bernadette's answers:
"The body, erect or bent forward?"

"Erect...without being stiff."

"Was the head inclined to one side or bent forward?"

"Erect also."

"What about the hands? How did she join them when
she said: 'I am the Immaculate Conception?'"

Later the sculptor wrote the following:

> Bernadette got up with the greatest
> simplicity. She joined her hands and raised
> her eyes to heaven. I have never seen
> anything more beautiful...Neither Mino da
> Fiesole, nor Perugino, nor Raphael have
> ever done anything so sweet and yet so
> profound as was the look of that young
> girl, consumptive to her fingertips. ...One
> could not have the least doubt in the world
> about the signal favor that she had received
> (Letter of September 17, 1863; D 7. p. 280,
> no. 1500).

Inspiration came to him at that moment.

Anxious for the contract, the sculptor goes to the
grotto with Bernadette. In the niche he does a silhouette
on paper to determine the size and position of the statue.
He also shows Bernadette "a portfolio of illustrations in
which the Holy Virgin is depicted in all sorts of ways"....
Bernadette scarcely paid any attention to them. Then, all
of a sudden, as we passed an engraving or lithograph of
the Virgin of Saint Luke, she quickly put out her hand and
said: 'There is something there.'"

This point, which has come down to us through two

traditions, has fascinated Picasso and Malraux. But they
disregarded, or were unaware of the contemporary
testimony, which tells us that Bernadette quickly added:
"But that's not it! No, that's not it!" (See H 3, p. 214, no. 83.)

Objections

In November 1863, the sculptor sends Dean Peyramale a
photo of his plaster model, which is about two-thirds of
the projected size of the finished work. Peyramale's letter
of reply suggests that Bernadette's criticisms had been
severe:

> The figure does not seem young enough
> and does not smile enough...The veil came
> straight down and was smooth...The hands
> were more closely joined, the fingers right
> up against each other; the left foot was a
> little more to one side, etc.

Aware of the great gap between Bernadette's vision
and that of the artist, and anxious to respect the latter's
freedom, Peyramale adds the following words that give
him a clear field:

> I do not know whether the rules of art will
> permit you to pay heed to all these
> observations. I am convinced that you,
> inspired by your talent and the Immaculate
> Virgin, will present us with a remarkable
> work of art (D 7, p. 309, no. 1543).

The case containing the statue arrives in Lourdes on
March 30, 1864, five days before the solemn ceremony of
its inauguration. Bernadette is recovering from another
bout of illness. She is beginning to get back to her games
and her routine. She is summoned away from her play
with the little girls and presented to Father Ollivier, a
preacher in Notre-Dame. In his presence Dean Peyramale

rebukes her, acting on the accustomed principle that
"humiliation is good for people." She is with the two
priests, looking at the statue which has been set up on a
piece of furniture in the next room: "Is that it?" asks
Peyramale.

Father Ollivier tells us that Peyramale questioned
Bernadette with "a bit of uneasiness," as they all stood
before the glistening Carrara marble. Peyramale realized
only too well that he would not be able to reconcile both
the shepherdess and the sculptor. In a letter dated
November 30, 1863, he had prepared the sculptor for the
ultimate trial:

> I seriously doubt that when Bernadette
> sees your statue, no matter how amazed
> she may be (sic!), she will exclaim: It's her!
> You won't take offence...

Programmed to be submissive, Bernadette tries to
give the desired response: "That's it..."

But she does not know how to pretend. After a
moment of silence she continues in a tone of regret,
"almost of pity": "No, that's not it!" (Memorandum of
Ollivier; SEMPÉ, p. 224).

The problem with the statue was the workmanship.
According to Bernadette, the characteristics of the Virgin
were simplicity, plainness, symmetry, and straightness.
The sculptor fancied her up too much. He whimsically
complicated the folds of her veil and her dress. He bent
the head back a bit towards heaven, though Bernadette
had insisted that it be straight and erect on her shoulders.

"She raised her eyes, but not her head. He has given
her goiter!" protested Bernadette.

The sculptor had added all sorts of slack lines and
folds. He had not respected the small size of the
apparition. The niche had been cleared, the rosebush was
gone, and he had room for a taller figure. The statue
should have been the same height as Bernadette—1 m.40
[about 4 1/2']. He had made it 1 m.70 [about 5 1/2'] (H 3,
pp. 152-156). In addition, he had not respected the

youthfulness of the apparition as Bernadette had asked.
To her, as to her big sister, Teresa of Avila, the Virgin had
seemed "very much a child." Or, as George Bernanos put
it in his *Diary of a Country Priest:* "Younger than sin,
younger than the race from which she came."

There is no doubt that the sculptor had been sincere,
and that the spark had passed from Bernadette to him.
But it had not broken down the conventions which were
part and parcel of his academic outlook. "Art is
eloquence," he had said, when he was received into the
Lyon Academy. This eloquence betrayed Bernadette.

A Ceremony Missed

Neither she nor Dean Peyramale attend the inauguration
ceremony for the new statue. The Dean decides that she
is to remain at the hospice, so as not to be subjected to
the curiosity of admirers at this triumphal ceremony. It is
also possible that he does not want an untimely remark
from her to prejudice appreciation of the statue.

But Peyramale is subjected to a dose of his own
medicine, because he too is kept at home on April 4, the
inauguration day. He is afflicted with a serious illness and
his brother, Doctor Peyramale, comes down to Lourdes
from Momères to be with him. The doctor notes his
impoverished state: "His whole fortune is 45
centimes...and there are the rents of 35 poor people to
pay" at the end of the month to prevent evictions such as
those the Soubirous had experienced (VÉDÈRE, pp. 90-91).

As for the artist, he himself admitted that in this
official triumph he experienced "one of the worst
annoyances" in his life "as an artist." Viewed from below
at an unaccustomed angle, where it was "lit up by an
unforeseen reflection of light," the statue showed "a
complete change in expression." The artist began to long
for the "polychromy of the ancients," and decided to have
the waistband painted blue.

For Bernadette, however, that day was the day of the
big decision which would involve the rest of her life.

Chapter 8

Bernadette's Religious Vocation

On April 4, 1864, after attending Mass in the hospice of Lourdes, Bernadette seeks out the Superior, Sister Alexandrine Roques.

"I now know, dear Mother, which religious order I should enter."

"Which one, my child?"

"Yours, dear Mother."

"Very well, my child, we will talk to the bishop about the matter."

Sister Maria Géraud, who had come to Lourdes for the inauguration of the new statue, "was convinced that Bernadette found enlightenment about this decision on her religious vocation in the Communion she received that morning" (PONev, 1202 v; D 7, p. 109).

Long Deliberation

In fact this decision was the fruit of long deliberation which was kept in the dark. The works of Dom Bernard Billet have shed light on the enigmas and apparent contradictions involved (D 7, pp. 79-128).

A letter of March 8, 1858 (published in D 2) adds a new piece of information. On that day the mayor of Lourdes had a revealing conversation with Bernadette. He proposed that she learn the craft of dressmaking or ironing at the community's expense. Her reply was: "No, I want to be a nun."

"But you may change your mind. In the meantime you should learn some trade," insisted the mayor.

"I won't change my mind. But I do want to do what my mother and father would like me to do" (D 2, p. 149).

Sister Alexandrine Roques, Superior, with Bernadette
(end of 1861—beginning of 1862).

Bernadette's first attraction was to the contemplative
life, according to the testimony of her two aunts,
Bernarde and Basile. She knew about the Carmelite
convent in Bagnères. Antoinette Tardhivail, her tutor, had
spoken enthusiastically about it as early as the spring of
1858 because it was the great yearning and drama of
Antoinette's own life. The latter would have liked to enter
that convent, but her health prevented her. She often
signed her name as "Sister Augustine," nostalgically
recalling the vocation she could not pursue. Did
Bernadette have an opportunity to speak to those nuns
through their black curtain or their grillwork? In any case
we do know that she made the acquaintance of a
Carmelite friar who had a great reputation for holiness
and musical ability: Father Hermann. But Bernadette soon
realized that her health would preclude such a choice,
even as it had in the case of "Sister Augustine." Being a
realist, Bernadette dropped all thoughts in that direction.
She turned a deaf ear to suggestions coming from that
quarter, even as she did to suggestions coming from
many other convents.

In 1860-1861, she spoke to Jeanne Védère, her cousin
who was the school teacher in Momères, about a
religious order named after her patron saint, Bernard.
She told Jeanne that she would like to enter it because
they practiced "vigils ... fasts ... strict disciplines ...
mortification." For a long time it was thought that
Bernadette had the Cistercians in mind. But a convent
dedicated to Saint Bernard meant the convent of the
Bernardines established by Father Cestac in Anglet, near
Bayonne. If informed of the matter, the founder would
have refused, partly because of Bernadette's health and
partly for another reason that he would not give to
Bernadette: "I don't want the world following after her"
(D 7, pp. 86-87).

Bernadette does not seem to have ever questioned
her desire for a religious vocation, but she did wonder
about the possibility of realizing it in practice. Her health
was one obstacle, her poverty another. She needed a

dowry, and there was no question of asking her family to provide one for her.

According to several witnesses, Bernadette was not attracted to the Sisters of Nevers. But before October 1860, she did in fact have an important conversation about her vocation with Sister Ursule Fardès, the Superior of the hospice. In a later letter Bernadette writes about that conversation in a lyrical tone that is exceptional for her:

> I love to recall the day we were at the
> wood house and you spoke to me about my
> vocation. How often I have thought about
> that little conversation! I can almost see
> you sitting on one step of the staircase and
> me on another. I glance at it every time I go
> there...(Letter of June 15, 1866; ESB, p. 190).

But we shall undoubtedly never know what she confided to Sister Fardès on that staircase, any more than we shall know what happened to Nathaniel "under the fig tree" (Jn 1:48).

Father Pomian tells us that "she would have liked the Sisters of the Cross." He may indeed have tried to point her in that direction, for he was involved with that congregation of the region. However, Bernadette reacted very negatively when these nuns coaxed her to try on the huge headpiece they wore in those days: "I want nothing to do with this tunnel" (PANev V, 1227).

The Sisters of Saint Vincent de Paul had no more success when they tried the same thing. They invited her to visit when Germaine Raval entered their order.

"I had quite a bad time of it, today," she confided, when she got back. "The day seemed awfully long to me. Those nuns tried their habit on me, but I did not feel at all attracted."

"Oh, that may mean you will have a vocation, Bernadette!"

"Oh, no! Quite the contrary!" (D 7, p. 89; note 516).

In 1863 the Sisters of the hospice pointed her in the direction of caring for the sick. It was to be a decisive

experience, according to Father Pomian, her confessor:
"She tried her hand at caring for a couple of old
people...fairly disgusting ones. She applied herself to the
work with charity and developed a taste for it" (A VII, p. 189).

We know a few details about one of these patients.
She was a "ragged woman, given to drink." She had
"fallen into a brazier, head first, and was severely
burned."

"From now on you mustn't take so many swigs," a
smiling Bernadette told her (BARBET, 1929 edition, p. 189).

Bernadette confided her attraction to Jeanne Védère:

> I love the poor a great deal. I love to take
> care of sick people. I will stay with the
> Sisters of Nevers. They gave me a sick
> person to take care of. When I am well, no
> one takes care of him except me. I will stay
> with them. (Letter of September 10, 1879;
> VÉDÈRE, p. 71; OG, pp. 192-193).

The problems that hold her back are the matters of
money and her health, and also the feeling of incapacity
imbued in her by day-to-day humiliations. In that era
people did not take due account of the bad aspects of
such an approach.

Bernadette is in this fix when Bishop Forcade of
Nevers comes to Lourdes on September 27, 1863. He talks
to her about her future frankly, as a former missionary to
the Far East well might. His adventurous past has taught
him simplicity.

"What are you going to be?"

"Nothing, I guess."

"What do you mean, nothing? One certainly must do
something here in this world."

"Well, I am here with the Sisters."

"Yes, but you are here only for the time being, aren't
you?"

"Oh, I will stay here forever."

"That's easy enough to say, but not so easy to do. Just
because they took you in for the time being out of

charity, you must not assume that they will let you stay here forever."

"Why not?"

"Because you are not a nun and you must be one to be admitted into the community once and for all...Here you aren't even a servant. In fact, from today on, you are what you said you were going to be just now: nothing. You won't last anywhere very long on that basis."

After a brief silence the bishop continued: "You are no longer a little child. Perhaps you would like to settle down in the world in some suitable occupation?"

"Oh, no, nothing like that!" Bernadette replied vigorously.

"Well, then, why not become a nun? Haven't you ever thought about it?"

"That's impossible. You know very well that I am poor. I would never have the necessary dowry" (FORCADE, pp.11-12).

The bishop seeks to reassure her: "When we recognize an authentic vocation in poor girls, we do not hesitate to take them in without a dowry."

"But the girls you take in without a dowry are skillful and smart, so they pay you back...I don't know anything. I am good for nothing."

"I noticed this very morning that you are good for something."

"For what?"

"For scraping carrots."

"Bah! That's not hard," exclaimed Bernadette with a laugh.

"It doesn't matter...They will certainly find some way to make use of you, quite aside from the fact that in the novitiate they will be sure to give you much of the training that you now lack."

"Well, in that case I'll think about it; but I haven't really decided yet" (FORCADE, p. 13).

In the following months Bernadette ponders the matter on the basis of these new possibilities. Her health goes through its usual ups and downs, but it improves during the winter of 1863-1864.

One of the things that Bernadette appreciated in the Sisters of Nevers was their prudent reserve in dealing with her, as compared with the active solicitation indulged in by other orders of nuns.

"I am going to Nevers because they did not lure me there," she would say later (PANev 1,547; see PONev 737 and 1110).

Thus her decision of April 4, 1864 was not the result of any sudden inspiration. It was the fruit of long deliberation.

Bernadette on Vacation/October 4-November 19, 1864

An unexpected pleasure awaits Bernadette in the autumn of 1864. She will vacation with her relatives for the first and only time in her life. The idea belongs to her cousin, Jeanne Védère, who comes to Lourdes with her father. Why not bring Bernadette back with them to Momères? Contrary to expectations, Dean Peyramale gives his permission on the spot. He himself is from Momères, and his brother is a doctor there. Given permission to go for two or three days, Bernadette will stay there seven weeks. The very next day Dean Peyramale takes a flying trip to Momères and entrusts his brother with the task of transmitting to Bernadette an unlimited "extension."

Bernadette does not escape the curiosity that dogs her everywhere. The first few days in Momères she sits in on the class taught by her cousin Jeanne. But her presence attracts the people of the area and class lessons are disturbed. It is better if Bernadette stays at home. Family life among her cousins delights her:

> Gay and playful, she greatly enjoyed chatting and bantering with one of her cousins (VÉDÈRE, p. 22; OG, p 177).

Mr. Dufour, a publisher in Tarbes, comes to Momeres. He wants to get even with his colleague and great rival, Billard-Perrin, who took a good number of photos of Bernadette in 1863. Dufour is doing quite well at selling pictures of Lourdes. In February of 1864, he had photographed Bernadette in the hospice and at the grotto. Now he is on a full-scale advertising campaign, and he wants to update his stock. He wishes to take Bernadette to his studio, and he has already had dealings with the bishop about the matter. Now he takes advantage of Bernadette's availability. He brings her to the Annet studio in Tarbes and takes sixteen negatives.

Bernadette is not at all upset by the absence of regular structures. Her order is within her own self. She is very precise in following her own little personal set of rules:

> She went to Mass every day and received Communion three times a week: Sunday, Wednesday, and Friday. Every day she made her visit to the Blessed Sacrament and said her rosary. When she prayed, one would have said that she was almost in ecstasy, she was so reverent and rapt in meditation (VÉDÈRE, p. 22).

François Soubirous comes to visit several times, just as he used to do when his eldest child was staying in Bartrès. It is he who finally decides when she is to return to Lourdes, though she is very happy in Momères. He prefers to see her nearby rather than far away.

The two cousins continue to exchange their thoughts about their respective vocations. This had been going on for some time, and they had discussed the subject at great length on April 4, when Bernadette had made her own decision. Jeanne Védère's religious vocation had been opposed by her family. She had been thinking of the Carmelites, but her father would hear no talk about the cloistered life. Weary of the struggle, Jeanne had resigned herself to a makeshift solution: "To join the Sisters of St. Vincent de Paul with the intention of entering the Carmelites later."

Bernadette's reply was direct and to the point:

Mind you don't do that! Stay at home
instead with your family. That would be
almost as if you planned to deceive people
and the good God too...But God is not
deceived. It is he who gives you the
attraction you feel...but it is not his idea
that you should enter the Sisters of St.
Vincent de Paul with the intention of going
elsewhere later...Be patient, you will
succeed (VÉDÈRE, pp. 65 and 68)

In Momères Bernadette is reported to have told her
cousin that the biggest difficulty would soon disappear.

This big obstacle was my poor godmother,
who was more opposed than anyone else
to my entry into the religious life. She was
sick at the time. Four days after my cousin
left, she died. That was on November 23
(VÉDÈRE, p. 88).

A Request Granted

Bernadette had left for Momères without having gotten
any response to her request of April 4. The reason is that
in Nevers the Superior General of the religious order,
Mother Joséphine Imbert, was hesitant. She was worried
that the celebrity of the seer would entail many
disturbances for any religious house she might join. But
the Mistress of Novices, Mother Marie Thérèse Vauzou,
was in favor of Bernadette's request. Sometime later she
would say to the novices:

It will be one of the great good fortunes of
my life to see the eyes that have seen the
Holy Virgin (PONev 1100 v; ESB, p. 181,
no. 48).

The bishop supports the request that he had provoked, accepted and transmitted. So when Bernadette returns to Lourdes on November 19, 1864, she finds good news waiting for her. The response is yes.

She breaks the news to her parents. She "made out that she was happy," noted her brother, Jean-Marie (PONev 147; D 7, p. 109; also see *Mélanges J. Coppin*, p. 78, note 40, for the correction of the date).

Her postulancy could have begun at once, but Bernadette's health suffers a relapse from the beginning of December to the end of January. She begins to get up out of bed only at the beginning of February, according to her letter of February 7, 1865 (D 7, p. 421, no. 1717).

Her convalescence is saddened by the death of Justin Soubirous, the little brother that she used to take to the fields to be breast-fed in the summer of 1856. He dies before he reaches his tenth birthday. The doctors who visited the Soubirous in the unwholesome atmosphere of The Jail had been right when they said, "If you want to preserve your children, you must not remain here."

A Marriage Proposal

On March 5, 1866, someone asks for Bernadette's hand in marriage. The suitor had already expressed his wish on April 20, 1863. His name is Raoul de Tricqueville and he is interning in medicine in Nantes. He directs his proposal to Bishop Laurence as if the latter were the father of the girl, morally speaking:

> It seems that there is nothing better for me
> to do than to get married, and I would like
> to marry Bernadette. If I am not permitted
> to marry her, I think I will quit this world.
> I would ask God for the grace to go off
> and die in solitude (D 7, p. 493, no. 1814).

We do not know what Bernadette thought about it, or even if his letter was conveyed to her. We only know, thanks to the suitor, that the bishop sent a blunt reply to his first letter. His request seemed to be contrary "to what the Holy Virgin wanted." But the persistent suitor will renew his request during Bernadette's novitiate in Nevers, sending his appeal to Bishop Forcade (FORCADE, pp. 38-42; L 3, pp. 236-240).

Bernadette begins her postulancy in February 1865. In April 1866, she draws up her petition to enter the novitiate (D 7, p. 196).

Delay

On April 28, 1866, Bernadette announces her departure (D 7, p. 498, no. 1822). But Bishop Laurence wants her to be in Lourdes for the inauguration of the crypt, the substructure of the "chapel" requested by the Virgin Mary. Sister Alexandrine writes the following note during this period:

> Bernadette...longs for nothing but the moment of departure. I fear it will be put off (again) if the Bishop of Tarbes demands that she remain here a while longer for the sake of the grotto. Pray, dear Mothers, that such will not be the case...so that this child will be safeguarded from self-love and from the covetousness of all the religious orders who come to solicit her, even in our presence...(D 7, p. 499, no. 1823; see p. 78, note 467).

This time Bernadette does attend the ceremony and takes part in the first official procession in response to the Virgin Mary's request. It is a joy for her, but it is also the occasion for many difficulties.

On May 19, the first day of the triduum, she is dressed in uniform and buried in the ranks of the Children of Mary so that she will not be noticed. On her return Jeanne Védère asks her to come out into the

courtyard of the hospice, where people from Momères
are waiting to see her. They quickly gather around her
and give way to exclamations: "Oh, what a pretty saint!"
    "The pretty maid!"
    "How happy she is!"
    That evening she must repeat the same performance
to get rid of the crowd that is gathering around the
hospice and trying to sneak in. They decided to parade
Bernadette so that the people will go away, so she is sent
to walk in the cloister for a few moments. The people
who manage to get that far try to touch her and offer her
souvenirs.

Jeanne Védère reports what Bernadette told her on
that occasion:

> How foolish they are! If they want objects
> touched, let them go to the grotto and
> leave me in peace (PONev 1234 v).

When Bernadette gets safely back inside, she complains:

> You show me off like some freak (D 7,
> p. 76, notes 450 and 452).

> You parade me like a prize ox (Anastasie
> Carrière, PANev 909 and PONev, 624).

Finally Bishop Laurence authorizes her departure.
However, it had been assumed that Bernadette would
make the journey with a fellow postulant, Léontine
Mouret. Now the father of the latter girl refuses to give
his consent. She is scarcely 17! They will have to wait.
Bernadette writes to the girl's father on May 26, 1866. Her
letter draws tears from his eyes. He permits their
departure (ANDL 42, 1910, p. 311).

Farewells

Spring 1866 is a time for farewells. Bernadette is brought
to Pau where her presence "draws so many people" that

"the police must be called in." On June 25 she goes to
Tarbes to say goodby to Bishop Laurence. But he is
making his Confirmation rounds and a letter must suffice.
She is also brought to Bagnères because Mother
Alexandrine had promised the Superior of that house—
on the condition that she would be discreet.

Bernadette also says farewell to Jean-Marie Doucet,
the sick little boy she visited on the Piqué farm after the
apparitions were over. Since the autumn of 1858 he has
been living on the Bourrié farm. He is now 15 years old.
Right now he is coloring some engravings of the
apparition and some portraits of the seer for Mr. Dufour.
He is also composing his illustrated memoirs.
Bernadette's visits will be the highlight of his story.

Billard-Perrin comes to the hospice to photograph
Bernadette with the nuns. He takes two snaps of her in
lay dress, one of her in nun's dress, and another of her
with the Children of Mary.

On July 2, two days before Bernadette's departure,
Viron gets permission from the bishop to do something
he has been requesting for a long time. He manages to
get three pictures of Bernadette alone. But the snap of the
maternal family is blurred, and that of the paternal family
is missing. There is no trace of it left.

Viron comes to bring the photos himself, wanting to
give them to Bernadette as a gift. She refuses.

"No, I want to pay for them. If you give them to me,
they will not be really mine" (ANDL 42, 1910, p. 311; D 7,
p. 125, note 193).

Bernadette gives the photos to her friends. She also
distributes all the little objects that still remain in her
wardrobe at the hospice. Then she makes her last visit to
the grotto. It affected her greatly, but there is none of the
excessive drama we find in certain accounts of the scene.
Aunt Basile Castérot, who shared the final evening with
Bernadette and saw her the morning of the day before
her departure, strikes just the right note:

> I was not there when she went to the
> grotto for the last time. I know that she
> suffered in leaving it, but she put on a
> brave front (PONev, 810 v).

On the evening of July 3, the whole family gets
together at the Lacadé mill for the farewell meal. It is
11:00 P.M. before they break up, an unusual hour in those
days:

> A large crowd was waiting for Bernadette
> outside our door; and when she went out,
> everyone pressed around her...to touch her
> (Anne-Marie Lamathe, proprietor of the
> mill, PATarbes, p. 315).

The next morning her closest relatives go to the
hospice for the final farewells. The group includes
Bernadette's father, her mother—"already ill" (A VII,
p. 287, no. 556), Aunt Bernarde, and Aunt Basile.

Bernadette is wearing a blue dress, a gift that is
forced upon her "by the Superior of the hospice." The
things she is taking with her are in a coarse linen bag of
multicolored stripes. Her trousseau is jammed into a
bulging trunk because in those days a prospective bride
or nun brought a lifetime of linen with her. Bernard,
Bernadette's youngest brother who was now six,
describes the scene:

> All of us cried. I did what the others did,
> not really knowing the reason for these
> tears (PONev 4, 831; D 7, p. 126,
> note 698).

"We cried, but she did not," specifies Aunt Basile.
Bernadette herself said: "You are dears to cry. I can't stay
here forever" (PONev, 810 v).

Lourdes Left Behind

In Tarbes they meet the Superior of Bagnères and her postulant, Marie Larretis. Aunt Bernarde, Toinette, and Sister Victorine, who accompanied Bernadette that far, remain on the platform with a group of friends and inquisitive people. Lourdes and its mountains fade away in the blue horizon amid a plume of smoke. That was the next-to-last farewell.

The final farewell takes place in Andrest (near Vic) where the Mouret family owns some property. Mr. Mouret thus manages to prolong his final moments with his daughter Léontine for a bit longer. It has cost him a great deal to part with her:

> A crowd of friends had come...They
> express a burning desire to see Bernadette.
> To satisfy them, Bernadette comes to the
> door of the coach. But the whistle is
> already sounding, and it is time to depart.
> There are tearful embraces and farewells.
> The train disappears, carrying the future
> nuns towards Nevers (ANDL 42, 1910,
> pp. 308-309).

Part II

Nevers
July 7, 1866—April 16, 1879

Bernadette, February 4, 1868.
Photo Provost.

The Saint Gildard Convent in Nevers.

Chapter 9

The Novitiate
The Trip/July 4-7, 1866

For the first and last time Bernadette boards a train and
leaves her native Pyrenees. Her keen senses take in all the
new sights she sees. To her friends in Lourdes she writes:

> Let me tell you about our trip. We arrived
> in Bordeaux at 6:00 P.M. on Wednesday,
> July 4. We stayed there until 1:00 P.M. on
> Friday. You can rest assured that we made
> good use of the time to go sightseeing.
> And in a coach, if you please! They took us
> around to visit all the houses of our
> congregation in Bordeaux. I assure you
> that they are not like the one in Lourdes.
> The main one, in particular, is more like a
> palace than a religious house.
>   We went to see the Carmelite church.
> Then we headed for the Garonne River to
> see the boats. We also went to the
> Botanical Gardens. There I saw something
> new. Can you guess what? Fish of all
> colors: red, black, white, and grey! I think
> the nicest thing of all was to see those little
> creatures swimming around under the gaze
> of all those children.

Bernadette, with a sympathy that was wholly
Franciscan, recognized herself in those little fishes. Like
them, she was an animal on display. Now, if she had her
way, she would abandon that role once and for all.

On July 6 they reach the second stop on their
journey: Périgueux. They leave there the next morning at
7:00 A.M. and arrive in the Nevers station that evening at
10:30 P.M. A coach is waiting for the two superiors and
the three postulants: Marie, Léontine, and Bernadette.

They lie down to sleep in the huge, silent house.
Bernadette can only imagine what her surroundings, now
shrouded in darkness, might really be like.

The Apparitions Recounted

At 1:00 P.M. the next day—Sunday, July 8—all the
novices and postulants are summoned to the novitiate
hall. All the nuns of the community, as well as nuns from
two other convents in Nevers, have been invited. For the
first and last time Bernadette will tell the story of the
apparitions to them, before burying herself in the silence
that she so ardently seeks.

To make clear the break between this last public
witness and the reserve of the religious life that she is
about to enter, Bernadette is permitted to wear the
peasant dress that has become famous through the photos
being sold to the public. In particular, she is allowed to
wear her white capulet.

The mistress of novices presides, alongside the
superiors who have come from the Pyrenees. Three
hundred nuns have gathered in the bay—the nuns of the
motherhouse plus other nuns from the town and the
surrounding area. The mistress of novices introduces the
seer, but in something less than flattering terms. She is
anxious to preserve Bernadette's humility. Bernadette
begins to speak hesitantly, first in *patois* and then in
standard French. She resorts to *patois* first almost
automatically, as if to protect herself, following the outline
of events that she has recounted so many times now:

> The first time I went to the grotto was
> Thursday, February 11. I went with two
> other girls to gather wood. When we
> reached the mill, I asked them if they
> would like to go see where the canal water
> joined up with the Gave. They said yes. So
> we followed the water of the canal and

found ourselves in front of the grotto,
unable to go any farther...

Then she describes the gust of wind and the
appearance of the lady in a white dress with a blue
waistband. When Bernadette gets to the muddy water of
February 25 and tells how she rejected it three times,
Mother Alexandrine Roques, the Superior from Lourdes,
speaks out emphatically: "You can judge from that how
little mortified she was."

Picking up the point, Mother Marie-Thérèse Vauzou
chides Bernadette amiably: "You were not mortified,
Bernadette."

"Well, the water was very dirty" (L 3, Vol. 1, p. 60).

Mother Vauzou doesn't like the idea of Bernadette
having secrets, even if they come from the Blessed Virgin.
She likes transparency in her novices. But she gets no
information from Bernadette about this matter.

Finally, Bernadette must also tell the audience about
her vocation. She is asked to describe all the headpieces
that were tried on her by other congregations of nuns.

"There was even one that bore the name of the
Immaculate," she notes.

"Our congregation was one of the very first to be
dedicated to the Immaculate Conception," says Mother
Marie-Thérèse Vauzou pointedly.

After telling her story, Bernadette dons the pleated
little cap and cloak of the postulant. At Vespers inquisitive
eyes will have a hard time identifying her among the
other forty-two postulants. Bernadette formally declared
that she had come to "hide herself," and her superiors
have exactly the same idea in mind. But the frequent
rings of the main doorbell of the convent make it clear
that this will be no easy thing to do.

Homesickness

As is customary, Bernadette is entrusted to a "guardian
angel": another novice who is to help her get used to her

new life. Her guardian angel is Sister Emilienne Duboé.
Bernadette feels homesick, as she will later admit in
order to help Valentine Borot get over the same problem:

> I was quite upset at the start. When I got a
> letter from home, I would wait until I was
> alone to open it because I felt I couldn't
> read it without crying out all my tears (L 453).

She overcomes her feelings of uprootedness not only
with courage but also with humor. To Lourdes she writes:

> I must tell you that Léontine and I passed
> Sunday watering the day well with our
> tears! The good Sisters encouraged us at it,
> saying that it was the sign of a solid
> vocation (ESB, p. 241).

Bernadette mobilizes all her resources to get
acclimated, including the following symbolic game
reported by Sister Philomène:

> She collected three stones in the courtyard
> of the novitiate. "Here are the companions
> of mine that I love," she said, showing
> them to us. On the first she had written
> "Lourdes," on the second "the grotto," and
> on the third "Nevers, Motherhouse" (L 17).

Her consolation is to go visit the statue of Our Lady
of the Waters at the back of the garden, in "a kind of
grotto," as she writes to the Sisters in Lourdes:

> It was there I could unburden my heart the
> first few days. Later our dear Mistress
> deigned to let us go there every day.

It was not really that Bernadette found any
"resemblance" there, as some have tried to intimate.
Rather, it was the open air of the place that brought back
to her mind the grotto, the gesture of welcome, and a
certain smile. The uprooting was hard on Bernadette. She

had never before left her region, her mountains, and the human atmosphere of the Bigorre province. She was attached in countless ways to those places where grace had blossomed for her.

She admitted that it was "a great sacrifice" (L 375), indeed "the greatest sacrifice" of her life (L 754). But she shouldered this new stage in her life without reservations:

> My mission in Lourdes is finished (L 391).
> Lourdes is not heaven (L 759).

Taking the Habit

With forty-two other postulants Bernadette dons her religious habit on July 29, three weeks after her arrival. She abandons her little cap for the headpiece with two white strips jutting down diagonally from under the chin. The exchange occurs during the ceremony itself. The postulants disappear into the sacristy and come back out with white bridal veils on their heads. Bishop Forcade then replaces each white veil with a black one, saying:

> You are going to receive a new name,
> which will remind you that you are
> separated from the world. You belong to
> Jesus Christ whom you wish to choose as
> your spouse.

For the first time the bishop gives Bernadette her new name as a nun, saying:

> Sister Marie-Bernard, may the Lord clothe
> you with the new human being created in
> God's image, in justice and holiness born
> of truth (Eph 4:24).

The mistress of novices had her keep the name of her patron saint in Baptism, Bernard of Clairvaux, but she had added the patronage of Mary. As she explained:

> It was altogether fitting that I give her the
> name of the Holy Virgin, whose child she
> is (RC, p. 30).

After taking their habit, the novices are scattered all over France. They will complete their formation in the field, working in each of the houses to which they are sent. It is a sound formula, associating the grass roots communities with the development of the young aspirants. It continues until it is prohibited by the Congregation for Religious.

An Exceptional Case

Bernadette, however, is kept at the motherhouse. Her superiors decide that it will be easier to protect her in that fortress than in any hospital or school open to all and sundry, where she may again become the prey of curiosity seekers.

Being treated as an exception is something that weighs heavily on Bernadette. She acknowledges as much when she tries to console Sister Emilienne Duboé, who is disappointed at being assigned to Clermont-Ferrand:

> How happy I would be if I could go
> somewhere to work instead of being
> obliged to stay here and do nothing!
> (L 24).

She appreciates the uniform that protects her from the inquisitive, particularly the veil that allows her to hide herself. She likes to pull it over herself and bury herself in it during her thanksgiving. But the novitiate does not foster complaisance. When Mother Vauzou makes a remark about it to her, Bernadette replies: "It's my little house" (L 28).

Who can blame her on that score? Didn't she come to hide herself? (L 29).

Deathbed Profession

Around August 16, 1866, Bernadette enters the infirmary;
but it is only a case of fatigue. In September, however,
her asthma is much worse. She is confined to bed, no
longer permitted "to go downstairs" (L 33). Sister Émilie,
the assistant infirmarian, is disturbed to see her "choking"
without uttering a word of complaint.

"It's as it should be, it's nothing," Bernadette tells her
(L 41).

As a precaution, someone keeps watch over her
during the night as people had more than once when she
was in Lourdes. Bernadette's chief concern is that her
attendant get some sleep.

"Take a rest in that armchair," she tells Sister
Eléonore. "I'll call you when I need you" (L 34).

Her detachment is complete and unreserved: "The
good God sends this to me; I must accept it"(L 35).
Confused by all the care and attention she is getting, she
remarks: "The poor are not treated like this" (L 50).

It is not that Bernadette is completely indifferent and
has no desires of her own. At first she was happy when
she was sent her companion in the novitiate, Léontine
Mouret, to help out in the infirmary. The infirmarian
made this choice deliberately. But soon another novice
appears in the infirmary in her place.

"Is Léontine sick?" asks Bernadette.

"No, but the mistress of novices has forbidden me to
pick her."

"Ah, I understand," replies Bernadette (L 48).

She cannot hide how painful it is for her to eat.
When Sister Émilie Marcillac brings in her breakfast plate,
Bernadette tells her: "It's my penance you're bringing me."

But she would take it without saying a word (L 42).
In her suffering she would look at the crucifix with an
expression "that spoke volumes" (B 2, p. 36).

When she was feeling better, she would laugh and
tease and even "sing a few verses in her Pyrenees dialect."

"She would laugh heartily when she noticed that I
didn't understand a word of it," recounts Sister Émilie (L 44).

Bernadette accepted the joy with the pain, saying:
"All that is good for heaven" (L 46).

On October 25, her condition grows graver. They
light candles before the statue of the Blessed Virgin.
Robert Saint-Cyr, the physician of the community, assures
them that she will not last the night. Sister Marcelline, her
room companion, is transferred to a room next door.
Mother Marie-Thérèse prepares Bernadette for death. The
chaplain, Father Victor Douce, administers Extreme
Unction to her.

Since Bernadette is going to leave this world, it is
proper that she make her religious profession on the
point of death. That requires a dispensation from the
bishop, but he is out making his rounds. When he gets
back at 7:00 P.M., he hastens to the scene in person: "I
don't want to give up the honor of receiving her
profession to anyone else."

The bishop himself offers the following account of
the whole scene:

> I find the sick girl out of breath, not to say
> gasping her last. She had just vomited a
> small basin-full of blood, and the basin was
> still there by her bed. I go up to her: "You
> are going to die, my dear child, and I have
> been told that you wish to make your
> profession. I'm here to receive it."
>
> "I can't pronounce the formula: no
> strength," Bernadette answers faintly.
>
> "That's no problem. I will pronounce
> the words for you. You need only
> respond."

It is with the poverty of a simple Amen that
Bernadette professed the vows that would link her once
and for all to God in the Congregation of the Sisters of
Charity. The bishop continues:

The Superior General...remained at the
foot of the bed with the pious intention of
closing Bernadette's eyes. I had hardly
gone out of the room when the dying
victim found her tongue again, smiled at
her Superior, and said: "You have had me
make my profession because you thought I
was going to die tonight. Well, I will not
die tonight."

There has been much comment and debate about
the rebuke which Mother Joséphine, the Superior
General, is supposed to have given Bernadette at this
point. Here is Bishop Forcade's account of it:

"What! You knew that you were not
supposed to die tonight, and you did not
tell me that? So you make the bishop come
here at this ungodly hour and get us all in
an uproar over you! You're nothing but a
little fool! I'm telling you that if you are not
dead tomorrow morning, I'm going to take
away your veil of religious profession.. And
I'll send you back to the novitiate with the
simple novice's veil..."
"As you see fit, my dear Mother."

Undoubtedly the bishop injected a note of harshness
into the conversation, which he did not witness directly.
One should assume a tone of humor in it and not take it
too seriously as a threat. There is clear proof of this in
the fact that Bernadette kept the insignia of her profession
and showed them to her novitiate companions with an air
of peace and joy.

"Thief!" Sister Charles Ramillon said to her, looking
at the veil and the crucifix lying on her bed.

"Thief or not," said Bernadette, ' right now they are
mine. I have them, I belong to the congregation, and they
cannot send me away" (L 54).

Although recovery from an illness nullifies a deathbed profession according to the provisions of Church law, the community hesitates to enforce this provision insofar as Bernadette is concerned. From the second month of her novitiate on, she had been ill constantly. They do not want to deprive her of the benificent security she is now enjoying.

"I've got it...It's mine," she says, showing the crucifix received at her profession to others.

"The good God didn't want me," she said to Sister Émilie. "I went right up to the gate and he told me: 'Go away. It's too soon'" (L 53).

She tells Sister Louise: "I am still too bad. The good God didn't want me" (L 53).

But God did want her mother. Louise Soubirous dies on December 8, 1866, during the Vespers of the Immaculate Conception. Forty-one years old, she had been used up by hard work, poverty, and nine childbirths, of which only four children are left.

"I could not express to you the pain that I have suffered," wrote Bernadette to Father Pomian. "I learned about her death sooner than I learned about her illness" (L 55).

A Time of Testing

Bernadette is well on February 2, 1867. She returns to the novitiate. Mother Marie-Thérèse Vauzou gets hold of her to make up for lost time.

"Well now, Sister Marie-Bernard, we are going to get into the time of testing."

"Oh, Mother, I pray you will not go too quickly" (L 69), replies the prudent Bernadette with a smile.

According to Sister Léontine Villaret, Mother Vauzou is also supposed to have said: "Now we are going to come down on you."

"I hope you will do it gently," Bernadette is supposed to have replied.

This response did not "edify" Mother Vauzou, Sister Léontine assures us.

Bernadette's novitiate companions bear abundant witness to her sober and solid piety:

Nothing distinguished her from the others except her regularity, her preciseness, her silence and, above all, her extreme charity...(Sister Joseph Caldairou; RC, pp. 71-72).

As for the tests and trials about which she is warned, the ones reported to us hardly go beyond playful teasing. Sister Stanislas recounts the following incident:

One day, while the rule was being read to the novices, Sister Marie-Bernard was sitting on a step next to the mistress of novices and mending the latter's apron. One passage in the reading dealt with the apparition of the Blessed Virgin to a shepherdess. At that point Mother Marie-Thérèse Vauzou turned to Sister Marie-Bernard and said: "That's how the holy Virgin always deals with shepherdesses, isn't it Sister Marie-Bernard?"

"Yes, my dear Sister," Bernadette replied amiably (L 91).

Another day there was a little raffle of a statue of St. Germaine Cousin for the novices. Bernadette won. Mother Vauzou is said to have made the following comment "in an ironic vein": "A shepherdess can't help falling into the hands of a shepherdess" (testimony of Sister Isabelle; L 91).

Still another day Sister Marie-Bernard was waiting for her instruction time "at the door of the mistress of novices." Sister Marguerite thought she detected a certain amount of fear in Bernadette (L 13). But Bernadette did not seem to be affected "when Mother Vauzou dismissed her" for her "fits of coughing" (RC, p. 83).

Other bits of testimony stress the happy side of their relationship. According to Justine Felat, "she seemed

content...when the main hall of the novitiate had been
made ready to receive Mother Marie-Thérèse. Ah, then
you could see her overflowing happiness sparkling. The
maternal air of our venerated mistress seemed to want to
draw all our hearts to herself and enfold them in her
bosom" (B 2, p. 51).

"One day when the mistress was returning home
from a trip," recounts Sister Stanislas, " we were waiting
for her in the cloister...When she arrived, Sister Marie-
Bernard rushed into her arms as might a child deprived
of its mother for a long time. Sister Molinery (Mistress of
Studies for the novitiate) said to Bernadette: "Well, well,
Sister Marie-Bernard. What enthusiasm on seeing your
Mistress again!"

"'Oh yes, my dear Sister,' replied Bernadette. 'It was
much too natural...I have repented of it'" (L 90).

These texts must be situated in the context of
nineteenth-century religious life. The novices often came
at a young age and from a very protected home
environment. They were inexperienced and they had not
yet been separated from the protective presence of their
own mother, in whose shadow they had been living. A
transfer of this maternal function had to take place in the
convent. And the maternity of the religious superior was
all the more important because it was a collective and
sacralized maternity.

In this atmosphere a basic differentiation took place.
Many young nuns found peace and equilibrium by
following the path of spiritual childhood. The strong
personalities, who stood out as the bulwarks of tradition
and the guiding spirits of the community, found a higher
equilibrium in exercising the responsibilities of spiritual
motherhood. The most famous model of this type of
Teresa of Avila. Unlike women in the world at that time,
who for the most part were restricted to the home and
passivity, these women had to make decisions, be
creative, govern, and travel.

The most difficult position was that of strong
personalities who, for a variety of reasons, never gained

access to these maternal functions and suffered from
nonfulfillment of their human potential. On the human
level this was undoubtedly the case with Bernadette.
Endowed with qualities that would have enabled her to
exercise serious responsibility, she found that her
exceptional status kept her in a protected situation. She
suffered from not fulfilling her human potential. And that
helps to explain why she died young.

The real trials of this period are the visits which
Bernadette cannot be completely spared, even though she
had come there to hide herself away. How could the
community refuse audiences to bishops, to members of
the pontifical curia, to important benefactors, or to Henri
Lasserre, who was preparing his *Histoire des apparitions*
at the request of the Bishop of Tarbes? If they wanted to
come off well when major requests were made, what
could they do but give their visitors the satisfaction of at
least seeing Bernadette. To this end they would give
Bernadette odd assignments, so that she would have to
walk past some area where the visitor might view her
from some hidden vantage point. Bernadette herself was
not fooled by all this. And since her orders were simply
to deliver some message or object, she would often evade
the visitor by taking a different route than usual.

On the other hand Bernadette did not seem to get
the connection between her presence in the infirmary
and the fact that the bishop himself would come to hear
the sacrament of Penance.

"How odd that a bishop should put himself to the
trouble of hearing the Confession of sick Sisters," was her
only comment (L 107).

Bernadette's "Blunders"

During this period Bernadette's gaiety gets her over the
trials and tests. She has a ready laugh and her "blunders"
as a novice give her many occasions to exercise it.

One day she is sent to get hot water in the kitchen.

There is no one there. She gets the water herself. In comes Sister Cécile, the cook, who is a "fairly rigid" woman.

"You should have asked for permission! Put that water back where you got it from!" (L 486), exclaims Sister Cécile.

The idea of "putting the water back in the tap" delights Bernadette. Her humor completely disarms Sister Cécile.

"There is that little snip of a nun laughing. A bigger one would have bawled her eyes out" (L 486).

Bernadette suggested to Louise Brusson that they should "teach a lesson" to a postulant who "often used to look at herself in the mirror of a little chest in the linen room."

"Write something to her on the mirror," suggests Bernadette.

"I got paper and pencil," recounts Sister Louise, "and I wrote: 'Better look at your soul.'"

This initiative is beyond the proper functions of the two novices. Mother Vauzou demands to know who the culprits are. Bernadette is the first to confess.

Another day they are in the refectory eating the hard circles of chopped carrots. Bernadette comes down on them a bit too vigorously with her fork and the carrots go "rolling the length of the table." The laughter was so contagious that "we couldn't eat any more," reports Sister Louise:

> At the end of the meal, Sister Marie-
> Bernard turns to me and says: "Let's go!"
>   I knew what she meant. So we head
> off to confess our fault to our mistress of
> novices (L 86).

On another occasion, according to Sister Madeleine, Bernadette was given the task of mending a headpiece "torn from one end to the other." She confides her troubles to the infirmarian.

"I will never be able to fix up this headpiece."

"Don't worry," replies Sister Madeleine. "I have some materials that are not in such bad shape. I'll give you one of them."

But the nun in charge of that work was not pleased and her rebuke was severe: "That's not the one I gave you!"

In the novitiate, it did not do to prefer intelligence over obedience. When Sister Madeleine tried to offer an excuse for her, Bernadette replied simply: ' I was in the wrong. I did not bring back the headpiece that had been given to me"(L 189).

However, Bernadette had no liking for those patching jobs, nor for the really worn out vestments that somehow fell to her to fix.

"Look, all they give me are pieces fit for the junk pile!" she said to Sister Elizabeth.

"Oh, your virtue doesn't go beyond that!"

Bernadette never assumed the pose of a statue that the age rather expected from a seer. When she arrived at the convent, she astonished the nuns with the question: "Do they jump rope in the novitiate?"

On being told no, she explained simply: "It's just that I love to turn the rope and make others jump" (L 14).

During one recreation period, the Sister in the kitchen challenged her teasingly to "drink an egg" that had been freshly laid. Before Bernadette has time to reflect, the two ends of the egg are pierced with a needle and she downs the egg. But right away she reconsiders the matter.

"Now I must go find the Assistant Mother and ask her for permission!" (L 270).

And she did.

Bernadette also has to laugh at her photos that are now on sale for ten cents. The price has gone down. She also laughs about her short stature. It gives her an opportunity to cheer up her companion in line, Sister Joseph Caldairou, who is one centimeter taller than she. They have fun making themselves taller and shorter, like two clowns in a circus. Bernadette has no complex about being short. Is it perhaps because the Virgin appeared to her in humble guise and seemed to be about her height? Bernadette has a taste for the picturesque, a gift for repartee, and a modest estimation of her own person. One day the person who is to give some word of edification, as provided by the rule, is absent. The others urge Bernadette to speak instead.

"I do not know what to say. I am a stone. How can you squeeze anything out of a stone?" (L 81).

In any case this humble response was uttered in such a way that Sister Stéphane Vareillaud never forgot it.

On May 16, 1867, Antoinette Dalias arrives in Nevers from Gers. She is eighteen years old. She will become Sister Bernard and one of Bernadette's many friends. The beginning of their friendship is almost comical. On May 19, the new arrival is talking to Sister Berganot.

"I have been here three days, and no one has shown Bernadette to me yet!"

"Bernadette? But there she is!" replies Sister Berganot, pointing to the girl next to her.

"This one here!" exclaims Sister Bernard, who had formed a "more elaborate ideal" of the seer.

"But of course, Mademoiselle, only this one here," replied Bernadette amiably. She would show real fellow feeling for Antoinette from that moment on (L 72).

Chapter 10

Religious Profession
October 30, 1867

On October 30, 1867 Bernadette makes her religious profession, her hands enfolded between those of Bishop Forcade. Sister Bernard Dalias tells us that her voice was "firm and without affectation." Sister Véronique, however, reports that it "quivered a little." She commits herself for life to practice the vows of "poverty, chastity, obedience, and charity."

The fourth and last vow was established in 1682 by Dom de Laveyne, the founder of the congregation. It was suppressed a little later, however, when Rome reviewed and revised the religious constitutions in accordance with the norms of canon law. Charity does not lend itself to canonical forms.

No Assignment for Bernadette

In the afternoon of the same day each professed nun receives what was customarily called "an obedience": that is, an assignment to some convent. Bishop Forcade himself presides over the ceremony in the novitiate hall. Bernadette's forty-three companions are called, one after the other. They are given a crucifix, a book containing the constitutions of the order, and their letter of obedience (FORCADE, p. 32).

It now seems that the bishop is finished. Has he forgotten Bernadette? She leans towards her neighbor, Sister Anastasie: "They give one to everyone...I would have really liked to do as everyone does" (PONev 624-625).

Now Bishop Forcade turns to the Mother General: "And Sister Marie-Bernard?"

Bernadette with the nuns, first in her peasant dress, then in the religious habit.

"Your Excellency, she is good for nothing."

Mother Joséphine says this, "smiling," points out Sister Caldairou, and in a low voice that can only be heard in the front rows (PONev 1297v).

When Bernadette approaches, the bishop says—this time out loud: "Sister Marie-Bernard, nowhere!" (PONev 533 v).

Then he speaks directly to Bernadette.

"Is it true, Sister Marie-Bernard, that you are good for nothing?"

"Yes, it's true."

"Well then, my poor child, what are we going to do with you?"

"Well, I told you that in Lourdes when you wanted to get me to enter the community, and you replied that that would not matter" (FORCADE, p. 32-33).

At this point the Superior General intervenes, as had been pre-arranged: "If you will, Your Excellency, we could keep her out of charity here in the motherhouse and give her some sort of work in the infirmary, even if it be only to clean up and prepare beverages for the sick. Since she is always sick, it would be just the thing for her."

The Job of Prayer

The bishop agrees and turns to Bernadette.

"I will try," she replies.

The bishop assumes a graver air and speaks out solemnly: "I give you the job of prayer" (PONev 1297 v).

The whole scene had been carefully planned and staged to resolve the following problem of conscience. They did not want to send Bernadette to a convent where she would be exposed to "the curiosity of the public." But the tasks in the motherhouse were regarded as the "top jobs in the congregation." Only in an exceptional case would newly professed nuns be assigned there. So they decided to give the outward trappings of humiliation to an assignment that might otherwise have seemed to be

a crowning honor. This is how Bishop Forcade himself
explained the scene to Count Lafond.

In the recreation that followed, Bernadette did not
show her wound. Her deeper sentiments can be glimpsed
in the encouragement she would give a bit later on to
one of her first sick patients, Louise Brusson. The latter
was confined to bed in the infirmary for bronchitis, and
she was "suffering a great deal from the mustard plasters
and the vesicants."

"Come on, my big Augustine," said Bernadette, "it's
for the good God. We must suffer for him. He suffered
enough for us" (L 116).

Mother M. T. Vauzou.　　Mother Joséphine Imbert.

Chapter 11

Bernadette as Infirmarian
October 30, 1867-June 1873

Now Bernadette is the assistant infirmarian, entrusted with
all sorts of small jobs. They range from taking care of the
flowerpots for the Blessed Virgin to taking care of the
night potties of the patients. She is used to the job
because she had been assigned to cleaning the toilets
during her novitiate. It poses no problem for her.

Taking Charge

She has a knack for the job of infirmarian, as she found
out earlier in Lourdes. Sister Marthe, the infirmarian, is
amazed to see how this little snip of a nun can take
charge of patients. A little "shh!" from her is enough to
restore silence (L 136). A single epithet, "Wastrel" is
enough to shut up Sister Pélagie, who has a hard time
controlling her tongue (L 137).

Her humor, air of authority, and advice create a good
atmosphere in the infirmary. She knows how to
empathize with her patients without going overboard. To
Sister Bernard Dalias, a compatriot from Gers who she
addresses in the familiar "tu" form, she says "My poor
Bernard, you can't take any more. You are half-cooked."
To Sister Dominque Brunet, who is excessively worried
about a prospective dental operation, she says:
"Mademoiselle, do you mean to tell me that you do not
want suffering?" (L 155).

Bernadette's arrival is right on time. Sister Marthe,
the infirmarian, is ill herself. More and more her work is
becoming too much for her. On April 12, 1870, she is
sent away for a rest. The infirmary does not suffer from
her absence. Bernadette is on hand to take charge of
things, and all goes well.

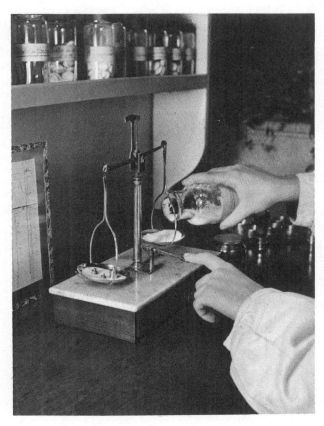

The Saint Gildard infirmary
with the dispensary used by Bernadette.

The infirmarian returns on July 9, worse off than
when she left. On December 23, her condition worsens.
The next year, March 22, the bishop comes to visit her. It
is a sign that her condition is desperate. She dies on
November 8, 1872.

Chief Infirmarian

Without any ado, Sister Marie-Bernard assumes all the
work and responsibility. She has no official title or
assignment, but she is in fact the chief infirmarian of the
motherhouse.

She takes pains to learn her job well, including how
to convert from one set of measurements to another. On
her infirmary notes she writes out some of the more
difficult conversions that we no longer are familiar with
today:

> 1 grain equals 5 centigrams
> 3 scruples or 1 gros equals 4 grams
> 1 ounce equals 32 grams

She stresses the importance of these calculations:

> Since a change in the position of the
> comma [French uses a comma in
> measurements where English uses a
> period: e.g., 1,32 instead of 1.32] may make
> a very big difference, it is very desirable
> that in the various formulas the amounts in
> grams, decigrams, centigrams, and
> milligrams be written out completely (ESB,
> p. 311).

To avoid any mistake, Bernadette writes down the
quantities in both measurements on the formula sheets
she prepares for various illnesses: e.g., spitting of blood,
dysentery, and scrofula. Here is her chart for the
treatment of rheumatism of the joints:

3 cups, infusion of elder.
Add to each 5 drops of aconite extract
(Alcorlature)
Aconitine liniment: 18 grains...1 gram.
Olive oil: 36 grains, 2 grams.
Hog's lard: 1 ounce, 32 grams (ESB, p. 312).

She has a sharp eye and initiative. When she notices
that Sister Angèle's chapped hands are bleeding, she says:
"You shame me with those hands. You must come to the
infirmary, and I will take care of you."

"Up there," reports Sister Angèle, "she put honey on
my hands, and a few days later I was fine" (L 161).

It was undoubtedly honey from beeswax cells. She
also treated Sister Angèle's eyes. And since the eyewash
made her cry, Bernadette said: "What! I give you one
drop and you give me several of them..." (L 164).

She insists on observance of the rule with a sense of
conviction that is a bit rigid, as was usual in those days,
but she also uses tact. The patients confide in her, telling
her not only their difficulties but even their dreams. Her
interpretation of dreams is not grounded on Freud or
astrology, but it indicates sound psychological intuition.
Sister Julienne Capmartin had been deeply troubled by a
dream in which the Child Jesus indicated some
dissatisfaction with her. On this foundation Bernadette
intuited a somewhat disordered affection for one of her
companions. The point struck home to Sister Julienne
(L 311).

The same Sister Julienne used to read her Children
of Mary book in bed, even though she had been advised
to stay wrapped up under the covers so as to perspire.

"So look there, a fervor woven of disobedience!"
remarked Bernadette. The book disappeared (L 313).

Sister Eudoxie tries to leave the infirmary without
permission and go back downstairs. Bernadette makes
clear her disapproval in such pointed terms that the
would-be free spirit is stopped in her tracks: "What am I
supposed to do?"

"Get back in bed and lie down! Sacrifice is worth more than prayer."

The next morning the patient was permitted to get up and to go back to the novitiate (L 305 c).

If she applied the rule strictly to others, she did so to herself as well. One winter day Bernadette found the infirmary to be too warm because the heat was up too high, so she opened the windows. The Superior General entered, was shocked to find the windows open, and severely rebuked Bernadette.

"Aren't you ashamed of yourself for doing that?"

"Oh no, my dear Mother!"

But a few moments later Bernadette "closed the windows and, fifteen minutes after that, went down to the community to confess her fault" (L 282).

Daily Life in the Infirmary

Bernadette's day in the infirmary usually began at 7:45 A.M., according to Sister Eudoxie Chatelain. First she checked the condition of the patients and served them the breakfast that was brought to them from the kitchen. She would move from one section of the infirmary to the next, having no time to sit down herself. Now and then she would offer a pious word of encouragement to the patients: "Love the good God truly, my children, that is everything" (L 304).

She is not reluctant to watch over the sick or to get up in the middle of the night to assist the temporary helpers assigned to her. Sister Clémence Crassan, who was trained in the work by Bernadette, testified that she had awakened Bernadette several times (B 2, 117-118). Bernadette told her in confidence: "I would love to take care of the sick in the hospices. I'm afraid my health is the reason that I have not been sent there. But I submit to the will of God. Let him do with me what he wills."

The Alarms of 1869

The bad side is the ups and downs of her own health. In 1869 she celebrates Easter in bed. According to her letter of April 6, 1869 (RSL, no. 21), 1968, p. 25, it was a violent crisis, but it did not last long.

In October of that year she is confined to bed again. Sister Cécile Pagès, who had been appointed to the infirmary in Paris, has to remain at the motherhouse. She gives us the following details:

> Bernadette at the time was in bed, spitting up whole basins of blood. I applied some vesicants to her. She said: "You can raise blisters all you want. I am as hardened to pain as cats are."

Things are going so badly that the subject of death is on people's minds:

> "If one sacrifices one's life truly, won't one go to heaven?" Bernadette asks me in the presence of Mother Joséphine Imbert, the Superior General.
>
> I reply gaily: "At least we would have one saint, for there is none in the congregation."
>
> Our venerable Mother replies: "You think there is none? Well, I think there are."
> "But not canonized!" I reply.

On leaving the room, the substitute infirmarian expresses her worry to the Superior General: "The doctor says that she could die in a fit of spitting blood."

Scholarly Disputes

Bernadette is on her feet on October 13, 1869, in order to give testimony on a delicate matter. The chaplains of

Lourdes have begun to publish a little history of the apparitions in the *Annales*. Public demand has prompted them to take this course because the history being written by Henri Lasserre is slow in coming out. The popular and familiar tone of the little history greatly upsets the writer, whose aim is to present a formal and dignified account. Lasserre hastens to Nevers to get Bernadette's criticisms of the little history, so that he may wield them against his rivals. He records her every little word of astonishment and denial, draws up a document in legal form, and has her sign it.

On November 16, Father Sempé, the chief chaplain, comes to Nevers to defend the work of the chaplains. Now Bernadette is subjected to pleas from the other side.

Insofar as the history of Lourdes itself is concerned, the arguments deal only with minute details, and in the end they contribute very little to the full historical story of the apparitions. But Bernadette now discovers all the human arguing that will surround the great event of her life. She also comes to realize how much she herself has forgotten. The experience makes a deep, almost traumatic, impression on her. She realizes that her every word will be wielded by one side or another in a dispute which does not matter to her at all. Her memory of the apparitions begins to grow blurred, just as the message about the procession had slipped her mind under Peyramale's savage reception on March 2, 1858.

Alarms of Death and War/1870

On April 12, 1870, the two infirmarians are confined to bed at the same time. Bernadette's condition again seems grave. Sister Honorine Laffarge tells us her impression:

> I go into the infirmary and I find that dear
> Sister in her death agony, so to speak. It
> seems to me that she has no more than a
> few hours to live.

"My dear Sister," I say to her, "our
Mistress has sent me to find out how you
spent the night?"
"Tell her not to worry herself. I will
not die today!" (L 160).

Sister Honorine saw the remark as a prophecy. The
fact is that Bernadette did begin to have remissions in her
asthma crises.

The Franco-Prussian War (1870) does not trouble
her. When the Prussians approach Nevers in the autumn
of 1870, Bernadette simply says: "I fear only bad
Catholics" (L 174).

In November of that year she writes:

They say that the enemy is approaching
Nevers. I could do without seeing the
Prussians, but I am not afraid of them. God
is everywhere, even among the
Prussians...When I was very young, I heard
people talking after Reverend Father had
given a sermon. They were saying: "Bah!
He's just minding his own business."
I think that the Prussians are also
minding their business (CROS 3, p. 223,
ESB, p. 279).

Death of Her Father.

That letter was the last her father received from her. A
short time later, Sister Madeleine Bounaix finds her
leaning against the chimney in tears. She had just
received the news that her father, François Soubirous, had
died on March 4, 1871. The date, March 4, was the
anniversary of the last apparition in the fifteen-days series.
François had been quick to travel to see Bernadette when
she was not home in Lourdes. But he never left his native

Pyrenees and he never came to see her in Nevers.
Bernadette does not hide her grief when she writes to
her sister, Marie, on March 9:

> My tears are joined with yours now. But let
> us always remain subject, however greatly
> afflicted, to the paternal hand that is striking
> us so hard lately. Let us bear and embrace
> the cross (ESB, p. 282).

It is in the same spirit that she accepted the war as a
sign of the time.

A Tribute to Her Intelligence

On September 3, 1872, she gets high tribute from Doctor
Robert Saint-Cyr, the physician of the motherhouse who is
also the president of the Niévre Medical Association

> An infirmarian who fulfills her task to
> perfection. Small and puny, she is 27 years
> old. She has a calm and gentle nature. She
> takes care of her sick patients with a great
> deal of intelligence, leaving out nothing in
> the prescriptions ordered. She also
> exercises great authority and has my full
> confidence (ESB p. 309).

These lines were written in response to questions
raised by a public statement made by Doctor Voisin, who
worked in the Salpêtrière asylum for aged and mentally
ill women in Paris. Doctor Voisin maintained that:

> The miracle of Lourdes has been
> sanctioned on the testimony of a child
> suffering from hallucinations who is now
> shut away in the convent of the Ursulines
> of Nevers (ESB, p. 309).

Her Peak Period/May 1870-1872

Bernadette has her best period from May 15, 1870 to the
beginning of 1872. She can write about her health
without any reservations:

> My health is quite good (December 25,
> 1870; ESB, p. 280).
> My health is terrific (1872; ESB, p. 316).

There are a couple of asthma attacks, but in January
1872 she can paint this reassuring picture:

> My health is only a little worse than last
> year. It is only the severe cold of this
> winter that gives me some difficulty. I have
> a little more difficulty in breathing.

Relapse

She suffers a relapse the following winter (1872-1873).
She is put in the Sainte Julienne wing of the infirmary on
January 17, 1873 (*Journal de la communauté*). On
February 3, she is still "very ill" (ibid; see L 318). There is
another relapse on Easter (April 13). She must "stay in
bed" for fifteen days (ESB, p. 321; see page 319).

On May 12, 1873, Mother Joséphine Imbert, the
Superior General, is able to take her in a carriage to the
Varennes orphanage. The visit of the two women is a big
festive occasion. But Bernadette is treated as a
convalescent and seated in a wheelchair. It is in that chair
that she utters her exhortation to the orphans:

> My children, have real love for the holy
> Virgin...Pray to her conscientiously. She will
> protect you (L 320).

On June 3, the relapse is more serious. It is at least
the third time that she receives the Anointing of the Sick

(*Journal de la Communauté*). Soon afterwards, however, she resumes her tasks. To those who are happy to see her up and around again she says: "They didn't want me at all up there" (L 325).

However, she is discharged from her job on October 30, 1873.

A Spiritual and Psychotherapeutic Resource

The step is not taken without regrets. Her position as infirmarian afforded an opportunity to send novices with problems to her, either to get care from her or simply to live in her presence. Bernadette's advice, simplicity, and stimulating vigor worked wonders. She was a spiritual and psychotherapeutic resource in the motherhouse. Even though she was a professed nun, Mother Marie-Thérèse would often invite her to participate in the recreation of the novices (B 2, p. 122).

One of her frustrations was that they would send her packing when Henri Lasserre's *Histoire des apparitions* was being read to the community. But what could they do? Hadn't the author made the Sisters promise that "Bernadette would never read this book" (B 2, 126-128)?

Bernadette was not fooled by these brusque dismissals. One day Julie Garros asked her why she was being dismissed so soon.

"Because they want to read something about Lourdes, they show me the door" (L 233).

On the other hand Bernadette was invited to recount the apparitions again on June 1, 1869, to four new arrivals. Again the point was made that no one was to speak to her about it again after that. Sometimes the exception does confirm the rule.

The community could make such free use of Bernadette because she herself was so strict about staying in her place and discouraging all signs of veneration or exaltation. One day the novices were just a bit too ostentatious in welcoming her after she had been absent for a long time. Bernadette was angry.

"Because you do me honor that I do not deserve, I will not stay with you during recreation."

Sister Clémence Chasan tells what happened next:

It was only with great difficulty that we managed to get her to stay. We had to promise to be more simple with her. Then she edified us all with her simplicity and her gaiety (L 272).

Her tonic laughter discouraged all affectation, as Sister Éléonore Bonnet learned at her own expense. To show off her beautiful voice, she sang a little song for the novices with just a bit too much fanciness. Bernadette's laughter was not appreciated.

"You intimidated me," protested Sister Éléonore.

"It's true that I did laugh," replied Bernadette, "but you will admit that there was a point to it" (L 265).

Francois Soubirous, Bernadette's father.

Chapter 12

Last Active Assignments
October 1873-December 1874

On November 5, 1873, Sister Gabriel de Vigouroux, age 28, is named infirmarian. Bernadette, now 29, becomes simply the assistant infirmarian once again. She had never officially held the chief job, though she had done the work. It is not easy for her to change roles because she has the infirmary well in hand. It is hard to move down from the top spot with its responsibilities to a subordinate role. When Bernadette offers good reasons for her viewpoint and way of doing things, the new chief infirmarian accuses her of pride (L 683). This may help to explain Bernadette's resolution at the end of her retreat in July 1875: i.e., to strive to become indifferent.

Lessons for Julie

In January 1874, she serves as assistant sacristan as well as assistant infirmarian. She dresses the choir boys and she washes and irons the purificators that have already been cleansed in three successive washings by the priest himself.

She also handles painful jobs in the infirmary. Julie Garros, her former companion and tutor in Lourdes, has entered the convent in Nevers. She is sent to the infirmary to be trained in caring for the sick. She recounts the following incident:

> One day Bernadette ordered me to take a walk with Mother Anne-Marie Lescure, who was blind.
>
> "You will take care of her as if it were the good God himself," said Bernadette.

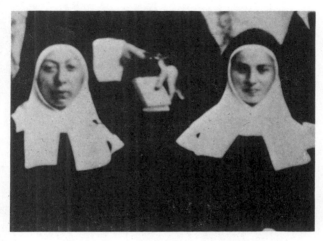

Bernadette and Sister Victorine Poux.

The Saint Gildard infirmary with the mortar and pestle
used by Bernadette.

"Oh, there's a big difference," I
replied.

I asked her why the patient did not
have on her full religious habit.

"You will come see this evening," said
Bernadette.

So I went and saw the sore of the sick
nun, crawling with worms that Bernadette
was siphoning off onto a dish. I could not
stand the sight.

"What a Sister of Charity you will
make! You haven't much faith," Bernadette
said to me.

The next morning I returned and
helped to dress the sick woman, but
without touching the sore. Bernadette did
the dressing very tenderly.

When the nun died on June 29, 1874, Bernadette
invited Julie to help prepare her for burial.

I didn't want to, out of aversion.

"You are a coward," said Bernadette.
"You will never make a Sister of Charity."

When the dead woman was dressed,
the Sisters came to embrace her. It cost me
a great deal to follow their example. I did
it, but it sickened me.

"A Sister of Charity who cannot touch
the dead! Who ever heard of that?" said
Bernadette (L 350).

Bernadette knew the kind of person she was dealing
with. Julie had a lively sensitivity but a temperament of
iron. Provocation and stimulation were good for her.
During the canonization process she displayed great verve
and joy in recounting that memory and other ones
relating to Bernadette.

It was Bernadette herself who put Julie's headpiece
on her the day she took her habit.

"All the ones I put on are solid," she said (L 289).

Julie remembers the words of advice that Bernadette
gave her on July 14, 1874, when she left the motherhouse
to exercise the functions of an infirmarian. Undoubtedly
knowledgeable from her experience at working in a
cabaret, Bernadette told her: "When you are in a room
with men, make sure that the door is always open" (L 351).

She placed great emphasis on caring for the sick:
"Always remember to see our Lord in the person of the
poor...The more disgusting the poor person is, the more
one must love him or her" (L 356).

"When you are taking care of a sick person...you
must withdraw before getting any thanks...The honor of
caring for them is sufficient recompense for us" (L 357).

It is on that note that the two friends part, never to
see each other again. Bernadette tells her: "There is no
need to give each other souvenirs when we truly love
each other...We must love without measure and dedicate
ourselves to our work without counting the cost...Let us
embrace now for the last time" (L 360).

"Accept sickness as a caress," Bernadette adds.
"Spend your all in the service of the poor, but prudently.
Never let yourself give way to discouragement. Have real
love for the holy Virgin."

Indifference to Affronts

Sister Victorine Poux visits Bernadette in September 1874.
She reminds Bernadette how the latter used to flare up
like a little savage back in the Lourdes hospice,
particularly in reaction to "little injustices" and "false
accusations."

"Now I am indifferent," replies Bernadette (L 368).

It is true. She proves it a short time later when
Mother Joséphine treats her and Sister Casimir as "useless
people." Sister Casimir gives way to tears.

"Is that all that's bothering you?" remarks Bernadette.
"Please be good enough to cut it out! You'll see a lot
more of it" (L 435; B 2, p. 180).

Bernadette moves towards a serenity grounded in obedience that has long eluded her and caused her much difficulty.

The confrontations with the new infirmarian, Sister Gabriel, were painful for Bernadette; but there was no rancor. In fact she makes an exception for Sister Gabriel in October 1874. She recounts the apparitions to her. Bernadette ends her account with the same words she had used to finish her written account of August 22, 1864: "She had blue eyes" (H 1, p. 61, line 500).

Bernadette in 1868. Photo Provost.

The Grotto of Lourdes established as a place of prayer and worship, surmounted by the basilica. When Bernadette saw a photo of Massabielle in its new form, she said, "My poor grotto, I don't recognize it anymore."

Chapter 13

In the Employ of Sickness
1875-1878

From 1875 on, the story of Bernadette's life is inextricably bound up with that of her illnesses. Henceforth "useless," she makes every effort to shoulder her new situation as a "job" in the service of God. "The job of sickness," she herself would call it.

Helping Others

It is a fruitful task because it is a good opportunity to send novices to help out in the infirmary. There they can profit from the witness of Bernadette, who always remains more attentive to others than to herself. She is a living sermon in her simplicity. As soon as her health improves, she finds ingenious ways to help out. She marks the pages in the books being read for the other patients (Sister Joséphine). She teaches Sister Rosalie, a novice, how to fold a veil. And her diagnoses remain keen. In 1873, when Julie Garros is discouraged and wants to leave—as this fiery and impatient girl often feels like doing—Bernadette chats jokingly with her to get her back on the track. But she is not so successful with Marie Champagnan, who enters the motherhouse on August 31, 1875, at the age of 19.

"She still needs her mother," says Bernadette to Sister Ursule Millien (L 378).

Events seem to prove that Bernadette was right. On September 14, the postulant leaves and goes back home.

When Sister Joseph Cassagnes is down with homesickness, Bernadette adopts the language of Jean Vianney, the Curé of Ars, to buck up her spirits.

"Don't you see that it's just the old devil...When he comes near you, you must spit in his eye" (L 416).

To Sister Casimir Callery, whose father dies suddenly amid upsetting circumstances, Bernadette says:

> Don't be distraught...The good God would
> not permit the parents of nuns to be
> damned. He gives them a special grace for
> the sacrifice they have made...My mother
> died on December 8, 1866. The holy Virgin
> wants me to realize that I should love only
> her and trust only in her...that she is to
> replace my mother...(L 433).

Return to Lourdes?

At the end of June 1876, a whole delegation from Nevers is on its way to Lourdes for the consecration of the basilica and the coronation of the statue. The travellers come to see Bernadette and get her messages and letters. She commends her family to Father Perreau, making special reference to her little brother, Pierre-Bernard:

> For them she did not want so much health
> and an easy life as virtue and the practice
> of their religious obligations...She regarded
> certain trials they had been subjected to as
> chastisements because, so she said, God
> could not bless those things (L 441).

Before leaving, the new bishop of Nevers, Ladoue, asks her whether she would like to go to Lourdes.

"Oh no, Your Excellency," she replies. "I prefer to be in my bed" (L 400).

To others she offers a dreamy reply:

> If I could transport myself in a balloon to
> the grotto and pray there for a few
> moments when no one was there, then I
> would gladly go. But if it is a question of

travelling like everyone else and being in a
crowd of people, then I prefer to stay here
(Reply to Sister Ambroise Fenasse,
Superior of the main hospital of Saint
Étienne; L 402).

On other occasions she makes similar remarks:
If I could see it without being seen (L 399).

I have sacrificed Lourdes. I will see the
holy Virgin in heaven. That will be more
beautiful (L 401).

Photos of the redone grotto cause her to exclaim: "Oh
my poor grotto! I would not recognize it any more" (L 390).

It is a sacrifice for her even to talk about it. One of
her visitors did not insist on pursuing the topic: "I got the
impression that we were causing her pain by dwelling on
the matter. We took our leave from her" (L 454).

Bernadette gives private messages for her parish
priest, Dean Peyramale. He is greatly upset over the fact
that he has been ousted from control over the pilgrimage
that he himself founded. Now he finds himself without
resources, faced with an empty parish church. When he
gets Bernadette's messages, he has a response sent to her:

Tell her that she is still my child and that I
give her my blessing (L 398).

The following year Bernadette learns of his death. It
occurred on Saturday, September 8, 1877, the feast of the
Birth of Our Lady. The news is brought by messenger to
the convent. Sister Nathalie Portat conveys it to
Bernadette, who is praying in the church loft. Bernadette
sheds tears for Dean Peyramale too.

Health Report/1875-1877

During these years Bernadette's state of illness continues,
with the disturbing ups and downs that typify her

condition. It is the very warp and woof of her existence.

In 1875 she keeps to her bed from April to mid-June (GUYNOT, 1936, p. 201), is back on her feet during the summer, and suffers a relapse in October *(Journal de la communauté)*. On November 19, an attack of blood-spitting raises fears for her life. She remains in bed until May 1876. The fine weather gives her new life. In June she attends Mass on Sunday, something which she has missed for six months (ESB, p. 475). But she can only get there by being carried (Letter of June 27, 1876; ESB, p. 428).

Her stomach seems averse to nourishment. She is "always broken-down," she admits in her letter of June 25, 1876 to Mother Alexandrine Roques. Such an admission is unusual for her because she tends to talk only about the bright side of things and her optimism vis-a-vis the future (ESB, p. 424). She employs her strength as much as she can. In August 1876, for example, Sister Joseph Biermann finds her sweeping the infirmary. She takes away Bernadette's broom, but the latter grabs it back.

"You shall not have it. Conquer or die" (L 413), says Bernadette jokingly.

Here we see the martial side of Bernadette's spirit, stirred by the military deeds of her godfather who won so much honor in the battle of Solferino. A book she was reading in the same summer of 1876 (title unknown) prompted her to make this comment: "Oh, this book makes me want to go off to war!" (L 417).

Her letters of August and September assure people that she is "suffering very little" or "not too much" (ESB, p. 434-436). But she cannot hide the fact that she is suffering from an incomparable weakness. She must cut short her letter of September 7: "My hand is trembling like that of an old woman" (ESB 437).

The same thing happens on September 13, when she is writing to Rachel Dufo: "I leave you here. I cannot hold my pen. I hardly know what I am saying to you. Adieu!" (ESB, p. 439).

Writing to Rachel, a girl from the upper middle class of Lourdes who became a friend after the apparitions, Bernadette switches between the formal *vous* and the informal *tu*.

Her November letters assure people that she is better (ESB, pp. 444-447). But it is always when she is feeling better that she writes to people. Here is the paradoxical side of her correspondence: although her health is basically going downhill, she informs people ordinarily of her improvement. And she stresses the good care that is being given to her, as if she were "a little baby" (ESB, p. 434).

A Letter to the Pope

On December 16, 1876, she is visited by the new bishop of Nevers, Bishop de Ladoue. Forcade had been made Archbishop of Aix in 1873.

"He is small and cold. He will not last long," said Bernadette after an earlier visit (L 338). In fact Bishop de Ladoue would die on July 23, 1877.

This time he has come to the infirmary because he intends to carry a letter written by Bernadette herself to Pope Pius IX. She writes it in bed, using a little wooden desk that is placed on her knees. One of her knees is in pain.

Her first draft is examined and revised as if it were a conciliar text. After all, this letter is for the pope himself. In it Bernadette had naively reiterated the remark that the bishop had made to convince her to write the letter: "The best way to get a blessing is to write a letter." One simply cannot expose the tactics of a bishop like that!

Moreover, Bernadette is too free and easy in her style. It was a point in time when the papal Zouaves (recruited mostly from France) stood out as symbols of loyalty and devotion to the pope. Bernadette had written:

> For a long time now I have been a Zouave, however unworthy, of Your Holiness. My weapons are prayer and sacrifice.

The thought is good and should be retained. It might well touch the heart of the Holy Father. But a little bit more modesty and formality is in order, like this:

> For some years now I have constituted myself, unworthy though I be, as a little Zouave of Your Holiness.

In her first draft Bernadette closed as follows:

> From heaven the most holy Virgin must often cast her gaze on You, most Holy Father, since You proclaimed her to be the Immaculate one and then, four years later, this good Mother came to earth to say: "I am the Immaculate".

> I did not know what that meant. I had not even heard the word. Later, after thinking it over, I say to myself: "The holy Virgin is nice. One could say that she came to confirm the word of our Holy Father."

Well, that ending is just a bit too abrupt. It will have to be stretched out a bit by adding a few more solemn phrases and qualifying adjectives. (That was hardly Bernadette's style, of course.) So the revised ending of the letter reads:

> I hope that...this good Mother...will deign once again to put her foot on the head of the accursed serpent and thus put an end to the cruel trials of the holy Church and to the sufferings of her august and well-beloved Pontiff.

A nun recopies the second draft on official monogrammed stationery of the congregation (ESB, p. 458). Then Bernadette writes out the letter again in her best handwriting, the little wooden desk still perched on her sore knee. She gets a little confused when she comes to the queer ending and jumbles it up a bit (ESB, p. 451).

And there are also spelling mistakes. That letter can't possibly be sent to the pope! She must do it over, despite her sore knee and her weariness. Somehow she manages to do it again, and this final copy is conveyed to Pius IX by Bishop de Ladoue (ESB, pp. 448-456). On January 14, 1877, he brings back from Rome the promised blessing.

The year 1876 ends badly for Bernadette, even though she writes as follows to Father Pomian on December 28:

> My stomach...not very obliging...has been keeping down a little more food for about a month (ESB, p. 473)

Yet the fact is that she has scarcely left her bed during the whole year, as she writes to Dean Peyramale that same day:

> Well, it is now a whole year that I am in my white chapel (ESB, p. 475).

She had only gotten out of bed for brief periods during the summer. And she left the infirmary only to go to Mass, with others taking her there one way or another.

A Marked Recovery/Summer 1877

A surprising improvement takes place during the summer of 1877. In a letter to Pierre Soubirous dated July 17, 1877, she writes:

> I take a walk in the garden every day to restore my strength (ESB, p. 486).

To Father Pomian she writes the following on September 15:

> My health has improved considerably. I can follow a great part of the community's exercises. I take walks and have a good appetite (ESB, p. 491).

She participates in the recreation periods once again
and goes around to the different groups, who love to
welcome her. During this period she walks well enough
to be given little messenger assignments around the
house. In September, with courage assisting, she manages
to climb to the second floor to see Jeanne Jardet, the
kitchen maid. The latter is sick and wants so much to see
Bernadette.

That same month she waits a long time in line for
Confession and "holds the place" of another Sister: Irène
Ganier. In October her good health holds up, so much so
that her companions lift her up (she is so light) to pick a
grape up high on the wall that had been overlooked
during the harvest (RC, pp. 84-85; L 477).

On the feast of the Presentation (November 21,
1877), she comes downstairs again for the renewal of
vows. And it is she who reads the pledge of renewal in
the name of the participants.

Winter/1877-1878

In December 1877, Bernadette is again confined in her
room. Her knee is the problem. But she does manage to
get up to help the novices with the Christmas crib. It is
she who places the infant Jesus in the crib: "You must
have been quite cold, my poor little Jesus, in the stable of
Bethlehem...How heartless the inhabitants of Bethlehem
must have been not to show hospitality to the infant
Jesus" (L 484).

But ill health takes over. Sister Ambroise Fenasse
comes to Nevers for the chapter meeting of January 28,
1878, at which Mother Adélaïde Dons is elected Superior
General. She finds "Sister Marie-Bernard immobilized on
her bed by a white tumor on her knee with a silicate
dressing" (L 499).

The silicate was an advanced treatment for that day,
according to Doctor Flament, but it is outmoded today.

On February 10, Bernadette suffers a relapse and spits blood (*Journal de la Communauté*). Again she must be watched over during the night. Her own concern, as always, is that her attendants get some sleep

"Don't trouble yourself so often," she says to Sister Julie Durand. "They think I am going to die. But I still have more than six months to go" (L 501).

Her asthma chokes her often and she needs air. But contemporary custom advises people "never to go to bed with the windows open because it is too easy to catch cold or to contract rheumatic pains." Bernadette is not easily put off. It is customary to open the window upon waking up in the morning, so she asks Julie Durand to do this "at 5:30 A.M." It is May of the year 1878, but even then Bernadette does not get away with it. Mother Vauzou passes by one morning and sees the open window.

"Foolhardy creature that you are! Why have you opened the casement window? To make your cold even worse?"

Sister Julie Durand hastens to close the window as Mother Vauzou departs. Bernadette stops her with a gesture.

"Wait! Our Mother did not say to close it. She simply scolded me for having had it opened" (L 505).

Thus we see that Bernadette remained a free creature. Her keen peasant casuistry, which we saw her use earlier with Julie Garros in the case of the strawberries, had not been forgotten.

The Last Summer

In September 1878 she is suffering a great deal from the worsening sore on her knee. However, she is able to go to the chapel to hear the words of the preacher who is preparing the community for the profession of perpetual vows. Somehow or other she even manages to kneel

down during the exercises. But she has to give the whole
thing up before the preparatory days are over.

"I can't handle it any more. I will not come back
again. I will remain in the infirmary," she says, towards
the end of the retreat (L 517).

She does come down to the chapel on September 22
for the renewal of vows, reading the formula established
in the new constitutions of 1870:

> I, Sister Marie-Bernard, wishing to
> consecrate myself to the service of God
> and charitable works in the congregation
> of the Sisters of Charity and Christian
> Instruction established in the diocese of
> Nevers, do hereby vow myself for the rest
> of my life to poverty, chastity, and
> obedience in the manner expressed in the
> constitutions of this congregation. I pray
> that Our Lord Jesus Christ, through the
> intercession of the holy Virgin, my good
> Mother, will give me the grace to fulfill
> these commitments faithfully.

After the ceremony she congratulates the singers for
their fine work:

> "I thought I was in heaven," she says twice
> that day. "If I were dead, I would be sure
> of my fate because the profession of vows
> is a second Baptism" (L 519-520).

> "Look for nothing better on earth" (L 529).

Her White Chapel

On October 30, 1878, the infirmary for professed nuns is
opened on the first floor, in the Sainte Croix room. It is
in the other wing of the motherhouse. Bernadette moves
into her final dwelling place on earth.

On November 12 and November 13 she is able to

come to the ground floor to meet the new postulants. She notices that one is down in the dumps.

"Are you feeling bad?"

"Oh yes, very bad!"

"Don't worry, you will persevere in the congregation," says Bernadette, putting her arm around her shoulder (L 530).

On December 11, 1878, she takes up permanent residence in her "white chapel," as she calls her big curtained bed. She has set up an image of St. Bernard alongside her bed.

"You pray to your patron, I see," says Sister Agathe.

"Oh yes, I pray to him well enough, but I don't imitate him at all. Saint Bernard loved suffering. I avoid it as much as I can" (L 410).

In an age when people talked a great deal, and rather wrongheadedly, about "loving suffering," Bernadette herself never succeeded in becoming a masochist.

Bernadette feels herself slipping into a new or second childhood. Her vigor, her memory, and her vivacity are weakening. She goes back to fashioning the little altars and religious decorations that she loved to make in The Jail and in the fields of Bartrès. One picture symbolized the Masses being said around the clock all over the world.

"I unite myself with all these Masses, especially during the night when I sometimes get no sleep," she says to Sister Ambroise Fenasse in January 1879.

But she does not want to end with a sad reminder of her sleepless nights.

"The thing that bothers me is this little choirboy who never rings the bell...I sometimes feel like giving him a good shaking" (L 500).

Immobilized, Bernadette uses her remaining reserves of strength as best she can. In August 1876, Sister Agathe had found her "sitting up in bed, shredding linen for rags." From Easter 1877 on, she spends a great deal of time painting or embroidering hearts. In accordance with the devotional practice of the epoch, she distributes them to different people with a gay remark.

> No one can say that Sister Marie-Bernard
> has no heart (L 462).

> If people tell you that I have no heart, tell
> them that I make them all day long (L 463).

In October 1878, Sister Thérèse Lacoste finds her coloring little images and sketching the crown of thorns around the Sacred Heart. With a mixture of mischievousness and seriousness she tells Sister Thérèse:

> If you want to be a nun, Mademoiselle, you
> must learn to love suffering. Our Lord
> gives his crown of thorns to his friends
> (L 529).

Good for Nothing

It is not suffering but inactivity that bothers her most.

"Always in the infirmary, always 'good for nothing,'" she says, reiterating the expression that came up in her first conversation with the bishop about her vocation and that was emphasized when she received her first official assignment.

She adds: "The good God has seen fit not to let me choose my own type of life. I certainly would not have chosen the state of inactivity to which I am reduced. I would really have liked to be actively employed at something!"

"You pray for those who do not pray," says Sister Victoire Cassou to her.

"That is all I have to do...My prayer is my only weapon. I can only pray and suffer" (L 515).

She had already voiced that theme in her letter to Pope Pius IX:

> My weapons are prayer and sacrifice, and I

will keep them until my last breath. Then,
finally, the weapon of suffering will fall
from my hand. But the weapon of prayer
will follow me to heaven, where it will be
even more powerful (ESB, p. 453).

Overcome by Joy

A breath of merciful grace enters Saint Gildard with the
arrival of Father Febvre in September 1875. Forty-three
years old, he replaces Father Douce as the chaplain in the
motherhouse. Bernadette had symbolized the austerity of
Father Douce in a little acrostic:

> **D**ouleur   (suffering)
> **O**ubl.   (forgetfulness)
> **U**nion   (union)
> **C**onfiance   (trust)
> **E**prouvant   (trying)

Bernadette softened the last item by replacing the
word *eprouvant* with the word *exigeant* ("demanding").
But now there is Father Febvre, who is encouraging and
helpful, just as Bernadette tries to be to others. Tact,
penetration, and docility to the stirrings of God are the
charisms of his ministry.

In October 1877, one of his sermons brings great joy
to Bernadette. Sister Casimir Callery reports the
conversation:

> "Oh, Seraph, how content I am!"
> Sister Marie-Bernard called me 'Seraph'
> because in the dialogue recited for the
> feast of our Mother Mistress, I was the
> Seraph. The name Casimir did not come to
> her because she had never heard it until I
> came along...
>   "What is it with you, then?"
>   "Didn't you hear the sermon?"

"Yes, of course."

"Well, the chaplain said that when one does not want to sin, one does not."

"Yes, I heard that. So?"

"So I have never willed to commit a sin. That means I have not!"

Joy lit up her face...I envied her happiness because I could not say as much (L 420).

Reproduction of a page from Bernadette's "Journal to the Queen of Heaven."

Chapter 14

The Day-to-Day Holiness of Bernadette

We have almost come to the end of Bernadette's life. She will soon undergo that mysterious passage to the hereafter, a trip that every human being makes with a certain degree of solitude. We can only view it "from the back," as one doctor who had studied the phenomenon of death and dying has pointed out.

Bernadette accomplishes this passage amid a series of mysterious trials and a dark night of the soul. She is not afflicted with suffering only. She also suffers from a dark night of faith and hope as well, as we shall see more fully in Chapter 16.

After the transparent light of the apparitions, Bernadette had returned to the normal state of faith in her daily life. But it was a sky lit up with stars, as it were. Now she enters a dark night without any stars at all. The final obscurity of Bernadette and her destiny links up with the initial obscuring of her early childhood; but it stands on a new level of silence, secretness, and poverty. For those who approached her, however, it was a night embodying the radiance of God. Perhaps it will also be that for us, as we follow her in the final stage of her life.

At the start of this book, we saw the invigorating and surprising light of the gospel message in the passion and suffering of her childhood poverty and her disdained social status. The final passion of her passage to the hereafter is even more luminous in that sense, but it is also even more secret.

Her Interior Axis

If we seek to glimpse the divine radiance in the daily words and actions of Bernadette described in these pages,

Bernadette in 1864.

then we must grasp the axis of her life. Hers was a day-to-day holiness devoid of superstructures, ideology, lengthy discourses, and any trace of complacency. Her holiness flowed from a basic inner orientation that gave unity to her life. We can lay hold of the starting points and end point of that orientation, even though her inner life is hidden in shadows and mist. For she followed the same basic line throughout her life: in sickness and in health, in the open air and the cloister, in moments of glory and moments of humiliation.

Her inner axis was glimpsed clearly by Father Febvre, her last confessor. The keenest of all, he was the best at recognizing and respecting her particular grace. This is what he wrote:

> When the humble Bernadette knocked at the door of the convent of the Sisters of Nevers...she already possessed certain lights, certain teachings, and a line of conduct that would give her direction and also help her spiritual directors and superiors to guide her on the pathways to perfection. Meditating on the words, recommendations, and secrets communicated to her by the Immaculate Conception and acquiring a deeper understanding of the mysterious actions she performed in the grotto, Bernadette would formulate rules of conduct that would enable her to arrive at the ideal of sanctity asked of her.
>
> Moreoever, like the prophets of the old law whose lives and actions were a visible confirmation of the great truths they proclaimed, Bernadette's mission would not just be to transmit the wishes of heaven. She would also practice works that gave expression to this message. Her habitual state of suffering would reveal to

souls the pathway and the necessity of
suffering for those who wished to be
"happy not in this world but in the next."
   In her heart Bernadette would feel the
same force that pushed her towards the
grotto in Lourdes to receive the visits of
our Lady. And these mysterious impulses
would be no less potent in driving her to
practice.

The words of Father Febvre are a bit lustreless. His
language, like Bernadette's own life, is wrapped up in the
narrow pigeonholes of the nineteenth century. We must
strip off the outer crust to get to the illuminating center
within. The wondrous Christian generosity of people in
those days was exercised in the framework of cultural
poverty and heavy juridical bonds. In the nineteenth
century, the congregation of the Sisters of Nevers,
founded under the evangelical inspiration of Dom de
Laveyne (1683), was submerged under the waters of
canonical legalism and a straitened concept of obedience.
Thus, during Bernadette's own lifetime, the order's fourth
vow of charity was suppressed by Rome because it could
not be reduced to canonical forms. Caught in the narrow
confines of this whole framework, Bernadette still
managed to grasp and hold on to the essential message of
the gospel and to link up with the basic inspiration of
Dom de Laveyne. That is the basic fact which Father
Febvre managed to see in his own way.

Father Febvre came to realize that the axis of
Bernadette's holiness was an inner one prompted by the
Holy Spirit. It was something imposed on Bernadette
herself, and hence on those who had the task of giving
her direction.

This inner axis was not just the corpus of words that
she heard from the apparitions. Her life and actions
welled up from a basic impulse rooted within. She did
not practice the message of Lourdes as one might
implement a rule or a law. The inner wellspring of all her

prophetic or mystical actions was love, and it was through love that she fulfilled the law. She did not rely on tiresome discourses or ready-made formulas.

This inner dynamism was hers prior to the apparitions. Long before, she had learned to grasp the gospel message at its very source. The apparitions at Massabielle would intensify and channel this impulse, and her religious life would help her to shoulder it even more.

Thus the axis of Bernadette's holiness is the message of Lourdes, but the latter is rooted in that prior, inner source which gave rise to Bernadette's actions as expressions of it.

Embodying the Message of Lourdes

The message of Lourdes is not restricted to the words Bernadette heard in the grotto: i.e., *prayer* and *penitence,* in the gospel sense of thoroughgoing *conversion* or *turning towards God.* It is to be found, first and foremost, in the *poverty* embodied in the very choice of Bernadette and in the immediate response of the poor to the good news. Jacomet, the police commissioner, bears unmistakable witness to this fact. Finally, the message of Lourdes is ultimately the very name and identity of the messenger: the *immaculate Mary,* the Virgin of the *Magnificat,* the prototype of the Church and of a radical and total living out of the gospel.

Here the apparition reveals its full meaning. Bernadette received a great deal from that encounter with the mother of Christ in the communion of saints that became transparent for a brief moment. The meeting took place in a concrete, visible form that Bernadette could understand on the basis of the tradition that had come down to her. The Virgin appeared to her as a living icon. Contemplating this woman, who was preceded and enveloped in a light "like that of the sun breaking through the darkness," Bernadette gained a better

understanding of what she was already living amid the
obscurity of faith. The various attitudes and poses of the
apparition—her prayer, her smiles, her sad glances—
reflected her compassion for sinners. The surrounding
crowd saw all these reflected on the face of Bernadette in
her transparent ecstasy: head erect, her face looking
upward. Bernadette simply modelled herself after the
Virgin Mary: the chief handiwork of God, the shaper of
Jesus' humanity, and the prototype of the Church.

When I finished the work of examining and collating
the chance words of Bernadette, I was greatly surprised to
see that they almost grouped themselves under the key
words of the message of Lourdes: *poverty, prayer,* and
penance. These are the lines of force that inspired
Bernadette's life. Her deeds blossomed from this interior
sap as the leaves of a tree blossom from within.
Bernadette, modest flower that she was, resembled the
model that she had always sensed near her and that
appeared to her in the grotto: *Mary Immaculate,* the
messenger of the Bible of the poor.

God Is Love

Once one has grouped the words of Bernadette around
the four themes mentioned above (poverty, prayer,
penance, and Mary Immaculate), there remains a final set
of words that are also important, indeed essential. They
relate to two other key words situated on the same axis.
One is *charity* in the fullest sense of the word (Greek
agapē): the unique love shared and communicated which
is the whole of the Trinity and of the Church. The other
word is *God,* or "God alone" (L 857), as Bernadette once
put it. These two latter words reflect the spirituality of
Dom de Laveyne, the founder of the Sisters of Charity of
Nevers. The first term, *charity,* is inscribed over the
doorway of Saint Gildard: *Dieu est Charité.* And the
formula *Dieu seul* ("God alone") is on the blazon of the
congregation.

However, Dom de Laveyne took these words from
the Gospel message, of which they are the very essence.
As far back as we know her, Bernadette was in full
agreement on this essential point. She always went back
to the same source. She knew how to scrape away the
surrounding mire to get at the core, even as she managed
to dig out the spring at the grotto.

The basic elements of the message of Lourdes—
prayer, poverty, and penitence—are the prelude to the
Gospels. They are inscribed in Mary's *Magnificat,* in the
preaching of John the Baptist, and in the message of the
Beatitudes. The other two expressions which sum up the
inner and outer life of Bernadette—charity and God
alone—are the very essence and epitome of the Gospels.
Thanks to the inner working of the Holy Spirit,
Bernadette brought all these values together almost by
instinct.

Thus we find an almost pre-established harmony
between Bernadette's own spirituality and that of the
congregation in which she lived her life. For according to
Father Ravier, the major themes which serve as an
inspiration for that congregation are: prayer, penitence,
poverty, service to souls, and charity towards the sick and
the poor (ESB, p. 223). They are the axes of Bernadette's
religious life too. Anyone will be able to recognize them
in her life and her deeds, and they need hardly be
spelled out here.

But we must go back one step further. These
evangelical axes are evident as far back as Bernadette's
childhood prior to the apparitions. They simply show that
her life was almost like a straight line drawn from a
single point. Her spiritual line was grounded on the
robust simplicity of her nature and the basic bedrocks
that gave her security from infancy on. The love which
pervaded her family life remained a profound source of
strength to her always. The trials which afflicted
Bernadette from the age of ten on, her struggles as a little
servant girl in Bartrès, and the poverty and disdain to
which she was subjected only helped to highlight a gift

that was hers always. She had received it from a living Christian tradition framed in the trappings of a certain time and place, and with a sure spiritual instinct she made it her own. Her instinct was rooted in her Baptism, and it flowed from there as water from a spring.

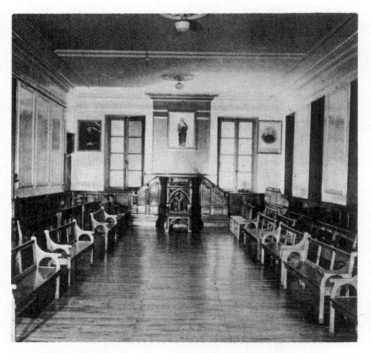

Novitiate hall, where Bernadette received her assignment.

Chapter 15

The Trials of Bernadette

We are now almost ready to follow Bernadette through the last months of her life. But before we do that (in Chapters 17 and 18), and before we consider the phases of her last dark night of the soul (in Chapter 16), we must pause for a moment to consider the crescendo of little trials that Bernadette faced every day in her life as a nun, right up until the end.

It is an important matter because it relates to one of the first messages she received from the apparition. And it was the most paradoxical and troubling message of all:

> I do not promise to make you happy in
> this world, but in the next (Message of
> February 18, 1858).

This eschatological promise orients Bernadette towards the ultimate realities and severs her from all human supports in this world. It is an abrupt promise evoking the *via negativa,* the dark night of the soul and the nothingness of which St. John of the Cross spoke.

So let us consider the little trials that formed the tissue of Bernadette s everyday life as a nun and prepared her for the final testing.

Lourdes So Far Away

The first trial in Bernadette's life as a nun, the one that drew tears from her the first Sunday she was in the Saint Gildard convent, was the uprooting from her beloved home territory and nostalgia for her Bigorre countryside—for the grotto especially. To be sure, she surmounted this nostalgia and regret, not only with determination but also with humor. Her tears watered her vocation and fashioned a rainbow at the end.

Given the tenacious shrewdness that was hers, and which was quite evident when she decided to leave

The grotto in 1858, washed by the waters of the Gave.

Bartrès and receive her First Communion, we know that Bernadette the nun could easily have gotten permission to return to Lourdes. At the very least she could have managed this on major occasions. She would have found no lack of supporters. and she knew how to make use of them if she wanted to. She was very good at coming to the defense of others. But whenever she was asked about returning to Lourdes, her answer was basically the same: no. Here are samples of her replies to people:

No, never! (to Julie Garros in 1871; L 195).

My place is here (L 405).

I stay in my little corner (L 408).

I have left Lourdes for good (L 510).

To return to Lourdes would be a very great sacrifice for me (L 375).

I am happy to remain here (L 510).

Go back to Lourdes? Oh, I will see Her in heaven (To Sister Ramplou in 1873; L 334).

Family Worries

The second trial, closely linked to the first, was her concern for her family insofar as she was the eldest child, the heir. Loyal to tradition and her social relations, Bernadette did not feel that she was now free of those bonds. She suffered over not being able to fulfill these deeply rooted responsibilities. She shared in the joys and sorrows of the family members. This was particularly true in the case of Toinette, who lost baby after baby. She tried to settle or smooth over family disputes, and she was anxious that her relatives would be faithful to their religious duties (L 406). Distressed that her sister should begin to engage in selling pious objects in Lourdes, she tried to dissuade her.

"I wrote to her, but, but she did not pay any attention," Bernadette confided to Julie Garros, her companion in the Lourdes hospice who had become Sister Vincent (L 198).

Later on, she would resign herself to the selling trade of her brother Pierre, but only on the condition that he would adhere to the prevailing precept of "not selling on Sunday."

"I don't ask that they be rich, but that they love the good God and be what they ought to be," she said to Sister Aurélie Gouteyron in October 1873.

The danger of getting rich through such selling bothered her a great deal. She was willing to accept their involvement in commerce, she told Father Perreau in 1876, who was going to see her relatives:

> Provided that they do not enrich themselves. Tell them right out not to get rich (L 406).

Inquisitive Visitors

The most irritating trial was undoubtedly the visits, which did not stop when Bernadette got to Nevers even though she thought the matter had been settled (L 662-663). In Lourdes she had faced up to all comers, not without chagrin but in the knowledge that she was the only one who could fulfill that particular task. For only she could tell people what she alone had seen and heard. But once the pilgrimage was established and authorized by the bishop, and once the chapel had been constructed, Bernadette felt that she had turned a corner in her own life. The pilgrimage to Lourdes no longer needed her, and so she had come to Nevers "to hide herself."

But that was a difficult, if not impossible, dream. A city set on a mountain cannot be hidden so easily (Mt 5:14). Her superiors were forced to make exceptions to manage the crowd, and in the end the exceptions were many. The

end of retreats was painful for Bernadette because the
retreatants "came looking for her as if she were a wild
animal in a sideshow" (L 768; her comment to Sister
Marie Delbrel).

After her death, Father Febvre and her superiors told
Father Cros about her "extreme aversion to parlors."

You almost had to drag her into one. When
you found her—she would go and
hide—you had to console her on the way
And she would keep saying: "Oh, how
tedious it all is!" (L 760).

Authority would have to be invoked because she,
with good reason, would point out her objection: "You
promised me!" Her obedience was not blind. She freely
expressed her own proper reactions.

One day one of the Sisters got permission for her
relative to see Bernadette. She invited Bernadette to come
downstairs, but she was honest enough to tell Bernadette
that she was not obliged to do this: "The Superior
permits you to do this, but she leaves it up to you."

"She leaves it up to me? Then no! No! No!"

And Bernadette headed for the back of the garden
(L 763).

Bernadette did not believe in carrying out duties that
were no duties at all. In that respect she was free from
the masochistic spirit of the time.

When she was performing the duties of sacristan,
some people came to observe her during a ceremony of
religious profession.

"Sister, where does Bernadette sit?"

"No luck," she replied, "today she will not be in her
regular place."

And with that remark she disappeared from the
scene.

In February 1871, Sister Victorine Girard arrived at
the motherhouse. She asked her neighbor in the novitiate
if she could show her who Sister Marie-Bernard is. Her
neighbor, none other than Bernadette, said that she

could. That was all she said. The next day, Victorine asked another nun the same question and was surprised to hear: "Why, you were right beside her yesterday evening" (L 179).

One day Sister Augustin Fort got the Superiors to promenade Bernadette in front of one of the convent towers to "show" her to a priest who was passing through town. Bernadette caught on to the trick and gestured to the offending nun: "Oh, my little one, you will pay me for this!" (L 64).

On another occasion Sister Julienne Capmartin was supposed to stop Bernadette on her way somewhere so that some people could see her. Sister Julienne improvised a little conversation about the flowers in the area. Bernadette, it seemed, caught wind of the trap. She kept moving on her way to the linen room, greeting Sister Julienne with only one remark: "Blabbermouth!"

On the other hand Sister Marie-Joseph Berger had more success with the same strategem. But in this case she was not presenting Bernadette to any adult or important person but rather to her little niece, age three. Bernadette loved children, and she stopped quite willingly. This was a real human relationship, not a peep show.

One day during a procession a woman picked out Bernadette, placed herself beside her, and could not hide her somewhat over-excited joy.

"I'm going to play a trick on her," whispered Bernadette to Sister Bernard Dalias. Bernadette slid between the wall and the bench and disappeared into the back of the chapel, much to the woman's dismay.

"You talked too much," said Sister Dalias to the woman (L 450).

Her superiors did all they could to protect Bernadette, but an exception was made for bishops passing through. They had a right to see her, and the list of those who did is probably far from complete:

Besides those who occupied the see of

Nevers—Forcade, de Ladoue (1873), and
Lelong (1877)—the documents permit us
to identify some dozen or so prelates.
Among them are Bishop Chigi, the
Apostolic Nuncio (L 128), and Bishop
Dupanloup (L 295).

"Those poor bishops would be better off staying at
home in their chanceries," said Bernadette (testimony of
Sister Marie Delbrel, L 766).

When she was told that Bishop Forcade had come
with some colleague to see her, Bernadette replied: "You
should say rather that he wishes to have me be seen by
someone" (L 765).

To spare Bernadette, efforts were made to show her
to people in seemingly accidental circumstances. Sister
Victoire Cassou recounts the following incident.

One day Bishop Bourret of Rodez had
come to Saint Gildard and he wanted to
see Sister Marie-Bernard. To do that
without letting Bernadette know what was
up, they decided to use a stratagem. The
whole community was assembled in the
novitiate hall. After he made a few pious
remarks, the Superior asked the nuns from
the Aveyron province to stand up. Those
from the Pyrenees region stood up in their
turn. Then the bishop went around so that
the nuns might kiss his ring. While he was
doing this, the Superior or Mistress of
Novices would say something about each
one of the Sisters...Well, Sister Marie-
Bernard caught on.

"Relax, I know just what I'm going to do."

With that remark, she disappeared
through a little doorway near her.

So I said to her later: "What about the
40 days indulgence? (for kissing a bishop's
ring)."

"My Jesus, mercy! There's 300 days!"
she replied.

Bishop Bourret, however, did not give up easily.
Indeed he had a revealing conversation with her in which
she made a surprising remark about the apparitions (see
Chapter 16: "Night and Fog").

Another bishop, almost certainly Bishop Léseleuc of
Kerouara, was admitted to the infirmary to visit a sick
Bernadette. He was struck with a more supercilious idea.
Playing negligently with his episcopal cap, he let it drop
on her bed. It was a "deliberate stratagem," designed to
get her to pick it up for him. Bernadette did not move a
muscle. The conversation drops to zero also. Finally, the
bishop takes the initiative: "Sister, would you mind giving
me back my cap?"

"Your Excellency, I did not ask for your cap. You can
pick it up yourself," was her reply.

In the end she had to pick it up out of obedience,
because a superior present in the room ordered her to
do so.

Fighting Her "Savage Nature"

Bernadette regarded the "struggle against nature" as one
of her most serious and difficult obligations. Readers must
remember that this fight against nature was highly prized
in those days, not without traces of artificiality. In
Bernadette's case, fortunately, her nature was solid and
resourceful. But she regretted what she regarded as her
savagely natural impulses.

"Oh, my impetuous nature again!" she exclaimed on
one occasion (L 772).

"Way down in there, we don't see what is going on.
We would not earn any merit if we did not master
ourselves" (L 773).

She also felt beaten at times: "I am discouraged" (L 774).

But those moments of difficulty rekindled the hope she
placed in prayer and the Eucharist. During one crisis,
when some thought her last day had arrived, she said:
"Don't worry. I will not die yet. The old human being
must die first, and it is still very much alive" (L 775).
    Bernadette was flexible in dealing with her
problems, however. "The first impulse is not ours," she
said to Julie Garros, "but the second one is up to us" (L 253).
    She accepted the fact that it would be a long-term
battle and prayed accordingly: "My God, give me
patience" (L 558). These trials led her to the cross, her
recourse in difficulties.

A Useless Servant

Bernadette was hurt a great deal by the fact that she was
not able to serve people as she wished to. This was all
the more frustrating because it seemed to go against the
very purport of her religious vocation. She did not really
mind being treated as a "useless" person or someone
"good for nothing" (L 499, 523, etc.). What bothered her
was *being* useless in fact, being unable to serve others,
and being frustrated in her desire to perform the tangible
works through which a human being finds self-expression
and fulfillment in his or her own eyes and the eyes of
others.

Severity of Her Superiors

The most celebrated trial, which has inspired the makers
of books and motion pictures, was the severity of her
religious superiors towards her: i.e., Mother Joséphine
Imbert, the Superior General, who died on May 1, 1878;
and especially Mother Marie-Thérèse Vauzou, the Mistress
of Novices.
    The trial was real enough. It was mentioned by many

witnesses during the two processes of beatification (L 3, pp. 168-175; and B 2, pp. 244-369). But it has been highly fictionalized and overexploited to suit the more mythological bent of the popular imagination.

The matter has been exaggerated on several levels and for various reasons. First of all, the severity of the superiors made a deeper impression on the other nuns when it concerned Bernadette, the seer of Lourdes, who was the object of discreet reverence on their part.

Second, the formal canonization process dwelt at length on all the minute details concerned with this matter. For it had a lot to do with such matters as obedience, the heroic practice of virtue, and even the "objections" against Bernadette's canonization that had to be resolved. If her superiors had treated Bernadette severely, then wasn't it obvious that she deserved such treatment for one reason or another? Excessive concern for all the minor details of convent life is typical in such instances. For example, the canonization process of Thérèse of Lisieux brought to light the quarrels between two rival factions in the Carmelite convent. The situation there was far less normal than it was in the Nevers convent.

Third and last, some people assumed for a long time that behind the acknowledged documents there were other documents buried away. Needless to say, the assumption was that the latter had a much more terrible tale to tell. This myth has been completely exploded by full examination of the materials. I shall not reiterate here what I have examined in great detail in several other works (see L 3, pp. 168-175); and *Bernadette vous parle,* Paris, Lethielleux, II, 344-394).

Here in brief is the whole truth, as far as it can be made out from these investigations. The severity of her superiors is a fact. But it was only a specific instance of a rule applied generally in that austere age. In some convents, far less well balanced than that of Nevers, the mistresses of novices practiced a veritable ritual of hazing that would shock us today. There were no absurdly

repugnant or brutal practices in the Saint Gildard
convent, but the superiors did try to break the self-will of
the novices in order to form them in obedience. The
testing was handed out in measured doses, depending on
the temperament of the novice in question. In
Bernadette's case, there was a more specific set of
motives involved. Her superiors were concerned not to
foster any elitist feelings in her. Her exceptional status
posed such a danger. And it was not just Bernadette
who "benefited" from a more demanding type of
treatment. Her superiors deliberately adopted that
approach because they had to guard themselves against a
displaced veneration for her.

These reasons seem to account fully for the attitude
of Mother Joséphine Imbert, the Superior General. She
humiliated Bernadette and treated her coolly for fear that
she herself might treat her with favoritism. One day, on
returning from Rome, she spoke a few words to each
novice as she embraced her. When she came to
Bernadette, she embraced her without saying a word.
According to the testimony of Bishop Forcade (page 26),
the Superior General treated her as a "useless person" or
even as "a little fool."

"Mother Joséphine! Oh, I'm scared of her!' (L 502),
said Bernadette.

And that is all we find in the voluminous dossier of
confidential remarks spoken under the seal of secrecy.

The case of Mother Marie-Thérèse Vauzou is more
complicated. Some of the trials she inflicted on
Bernadette were typical: e.g., kissing the ground. It was a
commonplace act of penance and humility in those days.

"I would look in vain for a floor tile in the novitiate
that I have not kissed," said Sister Julienne Capmartin
(B 2, p. 127). And Bernadette was not the only one to be
treated as a proud person or a fool.

The overall evaluations of the witnesses differ. "I
would not have liked to have been in her place," said
Sister Stéphanie Vareillaud, a fellow novice, at the
beatification process (PANev 327). On the other hand,

Sister Julienne Capmartin, who was treated with special severity by Mother Marie-Thérèse, had this to say:

> I never noticed anything resembling injustice or real harshness...She always treated Sister Marie-Bernard like the others—with no special consideration of course, but not unjustly either (GUYNOT, 1926, pp. 86-92).

What is clear is that Bernadette did have a certain fear of Mother Vauzou. And we can see an evolution in the latter's attitude towards Bernadette.

At first her dominant feeling was one of happiness at welcoming "the privileged child of the Virgin Mary," as she herself told the novices before Bernadette's arrival (B 2, p. 10). One day shortly after Bernadette's arrival, she had Bernadette go up to the dormitory early. Then she told Bernadette's story to the novices and reiterated that they were "highly favored to be able to contemplate the eyes that had seen the holy Virgin" (Testimony of Sister Cécile Pagès, B 2, p. 252).

When Bernadette seemed to be on her death bed and was formally professed (October 1866), Mother Vauzou said: "We are not worthy to have her, but one must do violence to heaven."

It was after that crisis, when Bernadette became active again (February 1867), that Mother Vauzou told Bernadette that the period of testing for her was to begin (L 69). Thus the severity was a clear and deliberate decision.

Undoubtedly there was an additional factor involved here: a certain disappointment on Mother Vauzou's part with regard to Bernadette.

"She is just an ordinary nun," said Mother Vauzou. The latter had a demanding conception of holiness that was centered on Christ. So did Bernadette, of course, but the conception of Mother Vauzou had certain mystical and heroic features that were quite alien to the humble pathway of Bernadette. The latter's way was the hidden way of the poor as described in the Gospels (Mt 11:25-27; Lk 10:21-22). It was devoid of great works, magnificent acts, and introspective ruminations. It was grounded rather on pure transparency akin to that of the Virgin Mary, the first and foremost of God's poor and lowly ones. That upset the orientation of Mother Vauzou.

Mother Vauzou did not see Bernadette raised to the altar as a saint. Sister Stanislas Pascal heard her make the following remark, which was accompanied by a "negative" gesture: "Oh! to lend my voice to the canonization of Bernadette..."

So long as Mother Vauzou was the Superior General (January 1881 to May 1899), there was no question of introducing Bernadette's cause for canonization in Rome. Mother Joséphine Forestier, who succeeded Mother Vauzou in the top post, was not unaware of this opposition. She came to submit the project of canonization to her.

"Wait until after I am dead," said Mother Vauzou.

What exactly was her complaint about Bernadette? Apparently it was that "insofar as nature was concerned, Bernadette displayed self-love." Sister Fabre discussed and debated this evaluation frankly with Mother Vauzou. But she could get "no other proof" of the charge except the following incident (L 682). One day Bernadette had improvised a little parable game, which was quite in keeping with her aphoristic bent. She drew a circle on the ground and said: "Let she who has no self-love put her finger in here" (L 682). When Bernadette put her own finger in to explain the rules, Mother Marie-Thérèse thought that she was holding herself up as an example of someone devoid of pride.

Bernadette certainly had no such intention in mind. Proud, sensitive, and even touchy, Bernadette had a militant concern for justice and was fully aware of being proud (L 683). Indeed she may have been overly conscientious about the matter, as her own words attest frequently. She knew that she would have to fight against this fault until her dying day.

"I have been rightly told that it [my pride] will die fifteen minutes after I do," she said to Jeanne Védère (B 1, p. 354).

The Reasons Behind Mother Vauzou's Harshness

The reasons behind Mother Vauzou's growing reserve and stiffness towards Bernadette seem quite clear. I should like to discuss them in some detail here.

1. She retained a relative amount of skepticism with regard to the apparitions of Lourdes. "All the same, the rosebush did not blossom," she said to Mother Bordenave.

In 1895 or 1896, she offered two other reasons to Canon Boillot, then the chaplain of the motherhouse, after he had just preached a moving sermon about Lourdes:

There are some bishops who don't believe it (PONev 1228-1229).

She specifically mentioned Bishop Dupanloup of Orléans, but his position is disputed by the various testimony we have (see L 295). The second reason she gave was this:

Oh! she was a little peasant girl...If the holy Virgin wanted to appear somewhere on earth, why would she choose a common, illiterate peasant instead of some virtuous and well-instructed nun? (PONev 1229; B 2, p. 357)

A few days later Canon Boillot expressed his astonishment about Mother Vauzou's view to three nuns on the convent board of directors. They replied frankly:

Don't you know that our venerable Mother is far from being carried away where Lourdes is concerned? She has spoken to us in very much the same terms (Ibid.).

At the same time, however, we must not oversimplify
the matter here. The fact is that she died with Lourdes on
her lips:

> She died uttering these words: "Our Lady
> of Lourdes, protect my death agony"
> (PANev 337v).

Her reservations were bound up with her classical
brand of spirituality. She was not keen on new devotions,
apparitions, and special charisms. Her rugged
Christocentrism (focused on the Sacred Heart) made her
mistrust the focus on Mary in popular forms of devotion.
In that respect she was ahead of her time. She stood for a
point of view that would be better known in more recent
times.

2. The second reason was the difference in class and
social status between her and Bernadette. Mother Vauzou
revealed this bias frequently, as Mother Bordenave and
many other witnesses testified:

> I do not understand why the holy Virgin
> should reveal herself to Bernadette. There
> are so many other souls more lofty and
> refined! Really! (PANev 327-328; other
> testimony in B 2, pp. 358-359).

3. The third and most decisive reason behind the
misunderstandings and stiff relations between her and
Bernadette was undoubtedly the following. She liked to
see great openness and frankness of soul in her young
nuns.

> She found Bernadette too reserved (PANev 225).

> She...judged the piety of her novices on the
> basis of the open revelations they had
> made to her (Mother Bordenave; PANev
> 327-328).

Mother Vauzou had doubts about Bernadette's

delicacy of heart. "She told me so herself," Mother
Bordenave confirmed (PANev 326). To Mother Villaret she
made the following remark about herself and Bernadette:

> Every time that I had something to say to
> Bernadette, I had the urge to speak
> harshly...In the novitiate there were other
> novices to whom I would have gone down
> on my knees before I would have done the
> same to Bernadette (PANev 1123).

This closing up was mutual. As Febvre rightly
noticed, Bernadette opened up only to "naive people like
herself," and to children especially. She "closed up with
persons who were not so simple" (ESB, p. 515).

The situation was made worse by the fact that
Bernadette did open herself up more readily to other
superiors. Sister Éléonore Cassagnes, in particular,
seemed to enjoy her confidence:

> Hence a little umbrage in the spirit of
> Mother Marie-Thérèse Vauzou (PANev 335).
> It also happened...that the venerable
> (Bernadette) confided her troubles to
> Sister Nathalie Portant, the second-assistant
> ...Hence a certain amount of hurt feelings
> (J. Garnier; PANev 1545 v).

In short, Mother Vauzou met not only the simplicity
of Bernadette but also the mystery that I have already
discussed. It was the mysteriousness of complete
transparency, which made her so delightful and admirable
in direct conversation and so alien to any analysis of the
states of the soul.

4. We must also take into account the impressionable
nature of Mother Vauzou, whose ideas were resolute and
rather fixed (B 2, pp. 361-362). She was somewhat
conscious of this, and she developed certain scruples
about having been too severe with Bernadette. During
one of her final retreats in Lourdes near the end of her

life, she talked this over with Father Jean Léonard, the
Abbot of the Cistercian monastery of Fontfroide. He
managed to reassure her on the matter.

"God deigned to let Mother Joséphine Imbert and I
be severe for Sister Marie-Bernard, in order to keep her
in the ways of humility" (PONev 104v, etc.), said Mother
Vauzou, two months before her death.

5. Finally, we must take due note of the artificialities of
the time. In those days naturalness, frankness, and
limpidity were not appreciated as they are today.

"A stiff, very touchy character," noted Mother Vauzou
about Bernadette in her secret file of the novices. But this
remark is compensated for by another, equally
confidential, remark: "Pious, modest, devout; she is
orderly" (PONev 324; PANev 334; B2, p. 364).

The trial was a real one for Bernadette, and deeply
felt, because the rich personality of Mother Vauzou
exercised a real attraction on her novices. She was
elected the Superior General of the congregation, and she
was regarded as one of the most remarkable nuns of her age.

Bernadette was delighted when Mother Vauzou
visited the infirmary. We have already noted how she
welcomed her back from a trip with an enthusiasm she
later regarded as excessive (L 90). Two factors reinforced
this sort of enthusiasm and spirit in the religious
community of that era. First of all, girls came into the
convent at a youthful age when they had not yet received
much training about life. Secondly, childlike
abandonment to their superiors was cultivated in them.
Regarding their superiors as representatives of God, the
girls projected a halo around them. They saw them as
visible signs and transmitters of God's will.

There was also some tension between the official
authority vested in the mistress of novices and the
charismatic prestige associated with the person of
Bernadette. To do justice to Mother Vauzou, we must
acknowledge that she never took umbrage at this. Far
from trying to destroy or eliminate the other pole of

attraction, she was wise enough to recognize it and use it for the benefit of the other novices, as we have seen. She was sufficiently sure of herself, accepted, and strong to feel no worries on that score. And the proverbial docility of Bernadette allowed for a *modus vivendi* which enabled her to exercise her attractiveness in a perfectly controlled way. But there was a certain amount of stiffness on both sides nevertheless.

In Bernadette's case, the stiffness was due in part to the fact that she did not always bend diplomatically as other novices might. Her mission had trained her to stand up to police commissioners, prosecutors, judges, priests, and others.

And yet there was a secret sympathy and a somewhat frustrated attraction between these two women who were so different in many ways. Let me cite one telling indication. When Bernadette was in the infirmary and Mother Vauzou was passing by outside (without going in), the latter would cough as a little signal; and Bernadette would reply with a little cough. This compensatory signalling attests both to their desire to communicate with each other and to the inhibitions which impeded such communication (L 281; B 2, pp. 129 and 352).

Now we must delve into the final and ultimate trials that were engraved on the life of Bernadette. They were both physical and moral trials. In the opinion of Sister Marie-Bernard herself, the moral trials were the most formidable and terrible of all.

Chapter 16

Night and Fog

From December 12, 1878 to the month before her death,
Bernadette would again be subjected to interrogations.
This time the circumstances would be particularly trying
for her.

Father Cros Encounters Obstacles

In this case, however, the historian and the friends of
truth cannot help but sympathize with those who inflicted
this particular trial on Bernadette, even though there
were good reasons for not bothering her again.

The case of conscience was posed for the first time
on August 24, 1878, when Father Cros showed up at Saint
Gildard. This Jesuit had been entrusted with the task of
writing an accurate, scholarly history of the apparitions.
The project had been dear to the hearts of the chaplains
of Lourdes ever since Lasserre managed to block their
own little history of Lourdes by marshalling Bernadette's
objections and sending a printed memorandum to
bishops and to the Holy Office in Rome

Father Cros was a devoted believer in Lourdes from
near the beginning He had met Bernadette in 1864 and
1865. Those very first meetings had given him the
inspiration to write a history of the apparitions and he
was ready to do it immediately. If he had, that might have
changed the whole face of the matter; for his genius as an
investigator would undoubtedly have tapped the
innermost wellsprings of Bernadette's mind and heart.
Unfortunately his superiors ordered him to finish his
history of Jean Berchmans first, a figure who was of more
interest to the Society of Jesus. So it was only in 1877,
after the death of Bernadette's parents and quite a few
other witnesses, that he undertook a systematic inquiry

Enlargement of the words of the apparition—
"I am the Immaculate Conception"—written in the patois by Bernadette.

among the surviving witnesses of the events in 1858.
There were still many around, twenty years after the
event. In the spring of 1878, Cros questioned more than
two hundred witnesses, including Bernadette's wet nurse,
her companions on February 11 (Jeanne and Toinette),
and the miller Nicolau. He vividly recorded their
recollections (CROS 1, pp. 509-520).

It was essential that he question the only witness to
the apparition: Bernadette. And, sad to say, in 1864 she
had offered on her own to give her account of it to him,
for a certain spark had been lit between them. He had
refused at the time, arguing that he believed her well
enough without that

So, on August 24, he comes to Saint Gildard in the
course of a bigger trip. He has already managed to get
around a thousand obstacles and to spirit countless
unsuspected documents from various files — including
those that the former officials of Lourdes in 1858 had
improperly concealed. He has met with success
everywhere. In Nevers, his gallant diplomacy runs up
against a stone wall. The nuns had been burnt by the
disputes over the earlier books and they feared a new
flare-up in the conflict. They now want to spare
Bernadette this new trial, as they had promised to do. The
clever keenness of the priest, which has worked wonders
so often, only tightens their defenses. The nuns refer him
to the bishop; the bishop refers him back to the nuns.
The runaround gets him nowhere.

Cros has managed to win the sympathy of ordinary
people. He has won to his side the bishop's valet and the
people in the post office. He has asked the latter to
inform him about telegrams, because he has asked the
bishop of Tarbes to telegraph an urgent support for his
project. It is all in vain. His last visit with the bishop's
valet to obtain some favorable response from the bishop
himself is a failure. All he can hear in the distance is "the
shrill, angry voice" of the prelate telling his valet not to
let Cros up.

He makes a last attempt with the Superior General:

"Pray that the holy Virgin may bend your heart."
     This is the response he gets: "My heart is not bent, it is upright."

Appeal to the Pope

It becomes clear to him that only an order from the pope himself can resolve the impasse. Cros had outlined his whole proposal as early as November 1877. In November 1878, Archbishop Langénieux of Reims brings it to Rome. On December 8, he announces complete success in his undertaking:

> Leo XIII had signed the papal letter in which he states at the outset that he would be indebted to anyone who would like to help to bring the project to a successful completion...or to give formal testimony as a witness (CROS, *Récits et mystères,* Toulouse, 1901, p. 12).

     So now Bernadette and her superiors have been invited to comply with Father Cros by the pope himself.
     Negotiations are resumed at Saint Gildard. The nuns, however, want to see no more of Father Cros himself. They are afraid of his passionately persuasive powers and his ability to pry into things. But they will accept Father Sempé, who was discreet, conciliatory, and modest in his requests when he came to give his side of the earlier dispute with Lasserre in November 1869.

Questions for Bernadette

It is Father Sempé who submits the questions drawn up by Father Cros to Bernadette on December 12, 1878. But her most frequent response to the fifty questions, which are divided into two parts, is: "I don't remember."

Uprooting and the passage of time have gradually erased the details in Bernadette's memory. Even as early as a few months after the apparitions, she had begun to forget dates and she could no longer distinguish what happened at a given apparition. The quarrels of the various would-be historians of Lourdes taught her how difficult it was to shed light on the details of events which one cannot go back to for verification. And her honesty can be gauged in the increasing loss of detail in her testimony over the course of time. Contrary to imaginary visionaries, who somehow manage to keep adding details to their message and the event surrounding it, Bernadette never added a word or a fact to her early testimony. She subtracts rather than adds. Having made the apparitions a part of her inner being, she no longer is able to objectify or describe them. She must summon back her memory from a painfully long distance, and it makes her dizzy to gauge it.

And yet certain memories do emerge now and then. Talking to Father Sempé, Bernadette remembers that she found the water "mild" when she crossed the Gave for the first time to reach the shore of the grotto (February 11, 1858). She can remember the prayers that she was familiar with at that point in time:

> The Our Father, the Creed ...in French, and
> the invocation "O Mary, conceived without
> sin" (B 2, p. 241).

What is easiest for her to recall are the words of the Virgin in *patois*, and she dictates them once again to Father Sempé.

The next day (December 13) Father Sempé comes back and finds her happy and relaxed. She recalls a memory from her early childhood:

> Her uncle, the husband of her godmother,
> returned from Betharram with a few little
> rings for her playmates. All the rings were

too big for the tiny fingers of Bernadette.
She was unhappy about this, but her uncle
consoled her by promising that he would
bring one that was her size. He kept his
word, but now unfortunately the ring was
so small that Bernadette could not get it on
her finger. Not discouraged, Bernadette
used her teeth to finally squeeze the ring
on her finger. But now her finger began to
swell and cause pain, and both the swelling
and the pain got worse. The ring had to be
sawed off her finger with a little file.

"I no longer had any desire for a ring
at all," said Sister Marie-Bernard, laughing
wholeheartedly (L 535).

Once again Bernadette repeated the words of the
apparition and they were taken down. But Cros is not
satisfied. There are still problems. He has objections
against some of Bernadette's abrupt responses. He is
upset by some of her lapses in memory and by certain
discrepancies on minute points, most of the latter having
to do with correct dates. Bernadette now talks as if all the
words had been spoken during one and the same
apparition, that of February 18, when Bernadette first
heard the lady's voice. Her proverbial stubbornness
resists Father Cros's arguments. Sometimes she is
perfectly justified, but sometimes she merely insists
stubbornly on her point of view as she has always done
when challenged. The inquiry goes on and on as
questions pour in from Father Cros, backed up by his
weighty arguments.

His requests now come to Nevers with the authority
of Leo XIII behind them. Each time the Sisters insist that
this must be the last interrogation. But finally, weary of
the struggle, they themselves submit the new questions to
Bernadette with no outside witness present. They do so
three times: on January 12, January 30, and March 3, 1879
(L 447-453).

Dark Night All Around

These interrogations entailed suffering for Bernadette.
Indeed she had made a surprising confidential remark to
Bishop Bourret of Rodez, when he had insisted on
meeting her on September 1, 1877. She told him how
reluctant she was to talk about the visions she had seen
when she was so young:

> All those things...are already so far back, so
> long ago. I no longer remember. I do not
> like to talk about them too much because,
> my God, what if I made a mistake. (L 461)

The remark should not astonish us too much. Such
forgetfulness and doubting are a classic phenomenon in
the case of mystics. It is difficult and often impossible to
recall the memory of those states which lasted but a few
seconds, of those fleeting moments of extraordinary
enlightenment. The Laplanders must find it hard to
remember the day-long light of summer during the
night-long days of winter. We ourselves often find it hard
to imagine that the sun will ever return when it rains day
after day.

Thérèse of Lisieux experienced the same eclipse
even more keenly. Giving way to vertigo and scrupulosity,
she thought that she might have "lied" after she had
recounted the vision of the Virgin that had cured her.
Bernadette never gave way to such vertigo. Her basic
conviction remained intact always. But she realized that
henceforth it would be better for her to focus her
attention elsewhere, to concentrate on her day-to-day life
and the future that God was gradually nurturing in her.
She would be happy "not in this world but the next," and
so she could no longer turn back to her past. In that
sense she was already focusing on the future life, and we
now view her "from the back," as it were.

The strength and evident clarity that had sustained

her in the face of all her challengers in the past was now
evaporating. She could no longer mobilize the lights that
had been hers. Like someone blinded in an accident, she
could hardly remember what it was like when she could
see the light of day.

But that was only a minor aspect of her trial, perhaps
the most superficial aspect of all. For now she is going
through a twofold dark night of physical suffering and
faith.

Cardinal Veuillot, who had expended so much
energy in the service of the Church, was crushed under
the weight of his final illness. It evoked this surprising
remark from him:

> Tell priests not to talk about suffering. Let
> them not speak about it! They do not know
> what it is.

Physical suffering is an incomprehensible night. No
one can talk lucidly and objectively about it. No one can
master it. Bernadette was wise enough to shoulder it
humbly, doing a far better job than intellectuals, wise
men, and scholars do. She was familiar with these dark
tunnels from her many attacks of asthma that brought her
to death's door. Yet, in the course of one of these crises,
she would say to Julie Garros:

> It is truly painful not to be able to breathe,
> but it is even more painful to be tortured
> by interior pains. That is terrible (L 345).

She said that sometime between July and October
1875. That is the first indication she gives of the deeper
purifying trial that marked her last years.

She came to appreciate the difference in degree and
depth between physical suffering and the deeper suffering
that undermined her practice of hope. She sensed the
dark shadow of the tempter near her. Her few comments
on the matter remind us of the Curé of Ars and Bernanos.
During the last few months Sister Tourriol heard her

speak to the spirit of evil firmly, though she was in much
pain.

"Go away," she said.

Her lucidity remained amid this dark night. When
she learned of Dean Peyramale's death in October 1877,
she said:

> Oh, now it will soon be my turn. But first I
> must go through *another death* (L 466).

Sister Marthe de Rais bears witness to the same line
of thought:

> One day I saw her in tears...I say to her:
> "Sister Marie-Bernard, why are you crying?
> Are you sick?" She replied: "Oh no! It's not
> that...If you knew all that was going on
> inside me...Pray for me (L 806).

This trial was known about quite early. Father Sempé
would bring the matter up the day after Bernadette's
death. Informed about it by Father Sempé, Jean-Baptiste
Estrade would mention the fact in his *Histoire intime des
apparitions,* which was first published in 1898:

> In the last years of her life, she was
> assailed by moral terrors, which were a
> thousand times worse than her physical
> sufferings.

Father Febvre, her last confessor, would specify the
most characteristic feature of this inner suffering:

> She often reproached herself for not
> having "paid back" God for all the graces
> she had received.

But this trial, too, is immersed in an even more
radical dark night of which we get only the most tenuous
glimpses. Like Thérèse of Lisieux, Bernadette experienced
a dark night of faith. Her life was no longer lit up by light
and alluring charms. Her fidelity now was to a hidden
and silent God, and it was shaken by the tumult of inner

doubts and temptations. Here again we see things only from the back, for we can barely glimpse her still lively freedom amid this apparent collapse.

The Passion of Bernadette

Bernadette's life ends as it had begun: in a "passion." In childhood she faced hunger, poverty, and health problems. Now she must endure sickness, impotence, and both physical and moral darkness. Here the word "passion" is correct in the strict, etymological sense, as her confessor makes clear in the following remark:

> The *passive* virtues abounded in her: a life of penitence sanctified by God's action ...and fashioned by the cross.

Commenting on God's mysterious work in her, he made the following relevant remark along the same lines:

> It is more that she was worked over than that she herself did the work (ESB, p. 515; B 2, p. 414).

Bernadette shouldered this "passion" (and she herself used that word) actively and consciously. With every ounce of strength in her, she identified herself with the passion of the crucified Christ. More and more she came to recognize herself in him, though only in a groping way.

"Our Lord was treated like a broken pot," she said as early as 1877 (L 481; B 2, p. 415).

Chapter 17

The Final Months
December 1878—April 1879

From December 11, 1878, Bernadette "is confined to bed
once and for all" (Lasserre, *Bernadette*, 1879, p. 349).
Henceforth she will get up only to lounge for awhile in
her armchair with its accompanying footrest.

A Vessel of Suffering

Father Febvre, an assiduous visitor during these final
months gives the following description of her ills:

> Chronic asthma, chest pains, accompanied
> by spitting up of blood that went on for
> two years. An aneurism, gastralgia, and a
> tumor of the knee...Finally, during the last
> few years she suffered from bone decay, so
> that her poor body was the vessel of all
> kinds of pain and suffering. Meanwhile
> abscesses formed in her ears...inflicting
> partial deafness on her. This was very
> painful for her and ceased only a short
> time before her death. After she made her
> perpetual vows (September 22, 1878), her
> sufferings redoubled in intensity and
> ceased only at her death. Her ambition,
> which she concealed as much as she could,
> was to be a victim for the Heart of Jesus (L 554).

Bernadette's superiors described in greater detail
one of her most obvious ills that greatly concerned the
infirmarians attending her:

Stairway to the Sainte Croix Infirmary.

Ankylosis of the knee... Terrible pain: a
huge knee, impaired leg, which one hardly
knew how to move. Sometimes it took an
hour to change her position. Her facial
expression changed greatly: she became
like a corpse. She, who was very energetic
in her desire for suffering, was completely
vanquished by the pain. Even while
sleeping, the least movement of the leg
drew a cry of anguish from her...and these
cries prevented her companions in the
infirmary from sleeping. She passed whole
nights without sleep. In her pain and
suffering she shrunk down almost to
nothing (shorthand notes of Father Cros,
(A l; ESB, p. 516).

Just "Holding On"

Doctor Robert Saint-Cyr, disconcerted by the ups and
downs of the preceding years, was further upset now. He
was all the more upset because he would have liked to
give her some relief. For he had a high opinion of her, as
his earlier evaluation of her work indicated. Frustrated by
his own impotence, he gradually comes to regard her as a
"queer patient." As a substitute for diagnosis, he would
say strange or enigmatic things to her.

"You have a terrible enemy," he said on one
occasion.

"With that," notes Bernadette, "he turned on his
heels. I'm beginning to think he's losing his grip" (Letter
of December 28, 1876; ESB, p. 473).

Finally, around the start of 1879, she makes a
decision: "I don't want him to come back!" (L 546).

She has such a hard time just "holding on" that she
avoids needless pain and effort. She does not try to rise
to the heights of heroic stoicism. She knows that she must

remain true to herself and not treat herself harshly. She
humbly accepts herself for what she is.

In January 1879, a nun offers her "thirty-six
recommendations" while asking her to pray for all sorts
of things. Sister Victoire Cassou recounts the incident:

> Bernadette did not let on anything, though
> at the time she was suffering terribly. On
> the contrary, she was very gracious to the
> visitor. But when the Sister had left, she
> could not help saying: "I like to see the
> back of people's heels rather than the tip
> of their nose. When one is suffering, one
> needs to be alone."
>
> I say to her: "You'll say the same thing
> about me after I have left."
>
> "Oh no, my poor friend, it's not the
> same thing" (L 545).

In a letter dated January 5, 1879, she tries for the last
time to reassure her family:

> I am doing better. I cough less since the
> weather has grown a little milder (ESB, p. 508).

> If I am cured, I would ask all of you to go
> to the grotto to give prayerful thanks (ESB,
> p. 508).

The Longest Nights

From February 1879 on, she must have a night
attendant to watch her in the Saint Croix infirmary: "her
right leg outside the bed, resting on a chair." The night is
filled with pain and continual groans, according to Sister
Michel Duhème, one of her attendants during those
months (L 551).

> It was a kind of muffled moan between
> clenched teeth, interrupted by brief

silences. I knew that she was trying to hold
it in for my sake...She was aware that I was
staying awake. To obey the assignment I
had been given, I said to her at one point:
"My dear Sister, you surely must need
something. Can I do something for you?"

"No," she replied, "go to sleep, go to
sleep. I will call you if I need something."

I tried to stay still to give her the
impression that I was sleeping, but she was
not fooled. When I said goodbye to go to
prayer, she said, "You didn't sleep, did you?"

Sister Infirmarian came to tell me that
I would not be going back to attend
Bernadette. Bernadette herself had told the
infirmarian, "I don't want that Sister to
attend me during the night any more...I
want Sisters who go to sleep" (L551).

Here we see a final indication that she still has her
inner freedom. She still can say: "I want," "I don't want."
She expresses it for the sake of others. and she does it
with enough authority to get compliance.

Incapable of stifling certain groans, she tells people:

Pardon me for complaining so much
(L 555).

Don't take my contortions seriously
(L 556).

An Inspiring Presence

Contact with her does not depress people, wherever she
may be and whatever state she might be in. A little
postulant, Camille Labaume, is brought to see her on
March 20. Bernadette is very ill, but she recovers enough
to say, "Mademoiselle, I am in a great deal of pain. I
cannot embrace you but I will pray for you."

She knows how to give a gracious thank you for the "fine broths" and the best wishes that people convey to her: "I am cared for better than a princess" (L 563).

On March 19, she informs Father Febvre that she has asked Saint Joseph for "the grace of a happy death." She doesn't want to hear any more talk about novenas for her: "To pray for my cure, not a bit of it!" (L 561).

The chaplain's encouraging words hit the spot and rekindle her hope: "Oh, yes?...That thought does me good" (L 579). But then she adds: "How long the end is in coming!" (L 578).

Extreme Unction/March 28, 1879

On March 28, they suggest that she receive the Anointing of the Sick. (This would be at least the fourth time since 1868.)

"I have been cured every time I received it," she protests (L 568).

After receiving viaticum, anointing, and some words of comfort from Father Febvre, Bernadette has a few words to say:

> My dear Mother, I ask your pardon for all
> the pain I have caused you by my
> infidelities in the religious life, and I also
> ask pardon of my companions for the
> many bad examples I have given
> them...especially for my pride!

The tone of conviction impresses all of them. Father Febvre noted that it was like the thundering voice of a preacher who wanted to make himself heard and understood (L 569; B 2, p. 269). Then they give her little commissions to carry out for them in heaven.

"Yes, I won't forget anyone," she replies.

On March 29, Father J.E. Greuzard brings her a photograph of a statue of Our Lady of Lourdes made by Armand Caillat, a celebrated Lyonnais artist.

"It is the least bad," she remarks indulgently. But she cannot help adding:

I don't know why people depict the holy Virgin like that. I have always said that she did not hold her head bent back like that. That is not the way she looked at heaven (L 571).

Giving Her All

At the end of March, Sister Philomène Roques receives permission to attend her at night. She hears Bernadette cry out in some painful nightmare.

"What's the matter, dear Sister? Are you in pain?"

"Oh, I was *down there,* and a little boy was throwing stones in the stream," Bernadette answers.

Was it perhaps the stone thrown by Jeanne Abadie that was now resurfacing in her final agonies?

That very morning a draw-sheet had to be placed on her bed. The infirmarian tells us:

Her poor body was just one big sore. There was no skin left on her lower parts (L 472).

As Easter approaches, she takes advantage of a final remission to decorate an egg. She uses a penknife to scratch a decoration on the rose-colored egg. Becoming a bit like her old self again, she reiterates a little thought that she knows will cheer up her visitors:

Human beings no longer have a heart, so I put one on eggs.

They cut her hair for the last time, as they had been doing periodically for the benefit of various mission works. It provides some money for the ransom of slaves. That explains her reply to Sister Marie Guerre one morning, when the latter took off her bonnet for the

morning dressing and found her head shaved: "It's to buy
a black woman."
    Bernadette never gave less than her all, and she did
it with a ready heart.

Holy Week

During Holy Week (April 6-13, 1879), the scabs and sores
become worse. Bernadette asks for some help:

> Look among your drugs...for something to
> revive me. I feel so weak I can hardly breathe.
> Bring me some strong vinegar to sniff (L 577).

The time has come for her to divest herself of
everything: she has all the images around her bed taken
away.
    "This is enough for me," she says, pointing to her
crucifix.
    On Monday, April 7, the questions and disputes of
the historians come back to her mind. She finds the
strength to make the following comments to Mother
Éléonore Cassagnes:

> As for me, I want no disputes. I certainly
> advised my relatives to stay out of it (L 576).

> I have told the events. Let people abide by
> what I said the first time. I may have
> forgotten and so may others. The simpler
> one writes, the better it will be. The
> passion touches me more when I read it
> than when someone explains it to me (L 576).

Chapter 18

Easter For Bernadette

On Easter Sunday, April 13, Bernadette "was coughing continuously." To Sister Saint-Cyr Jollet, she confides the following:

> This morning, after Holy Communion, I asked our Lord for five minutes relief so that I could talk to him leisurely But he did not choose to give me them....*My passion will last until my death.*

Farewell to Sister Bernard

On Easter Monday she is visited by Sister Bernard Dalias:

> The curtains had been raised. The patient's face was turned towards the wall, and she did not stir...I went to lean over the foot of her bed for a moment to see her one last time.
> Then, with one of those childish expressions she had always managed to keep, she opened one eye and looked at me, making a little sign that I was to come closer...Her emaciated hand touched mine lightly.
> "Adieu...Bernard," she said to me, "this time is really the last."
> Prompted by an impulse to venerate her, I was going to bring her little hand up to my lips; but she very quickly pulled it back under the covers (L 583).

Bernard Dalias was the girl who, when she was introduced to Bernadette for the first time, had said: "This one here!" She now recalls that incident:

Bernadette's "white chapel."

When we first met, Bernadette had
extended that same hand to me with a
smile. Today she was withdrawing it...Thus
our twelve years of tender friendship were
enclosed between two handshakes...She did
not notice the presence of my companions,
so that amounted to the privilege of a
personal farewell for me.

Ground in the Mill

That same Easter Monday she is still putting up a
fight. To Sister Céile Pagès, the house pharmacist, she
says:

There's no relief for me. Father Chaplain
told me that the good God wants me to
merit as much as I can while I remain on
this earth. I guess I must resign myself.

Her face is flushed, her prostration overwhelming. A
childhood memory flits across her mind.
"I have been ground in the mill like a grain of
wheat," she says to Sister Léontine. "I would never have
thought that one must suffer so much to die" (L 585).
That night (between Easter Monday and Easter
Tuesday) she enters a "spiritual agony."
"Get away, Satan," her confessor hears her repeat
several times. He recounts what happened next:

On Tuesday morning she told me that the
devil had tried to frighten her, but that she
had invoked the holy name of Jesus and
the whole thing had disappeared (L 586).

That same morning she received Holy
Communion again; but in the course of the
morning she was subjected to a serious

crisis of oppression. She had me
summoned and asked to receive the
sacrament of Penance. Afterwards I gave
her the plenary indulgence for the dying.
As I was telling her to renew the sacrifice
of her life out of love, she interrupted me
with a surprising liveliness: "What sacrifice?
It isn't a sacrifice to leave a meager life
where one encounters so many difficulties
in trying to belong to God (L 587)."

She makes every effort to repeat the
invocations I suggest to her. But she says:
"How right the author of the *Imitation of
Christ* was in telling people that they must
not wait for the last moment to serve God.
One is capable of so little!"

At 7:00 P.M. Sister Nathalie comes to her bedside.
She has a rare gift for making contact with people and
being a sympathetic presence, a gift which she developed
working with the deaf.

"My dear Sister, I'm afraid. I have received so many
graces and I have profited so little from them,"
Bernadette tells her.

Sister Nathalie encourages her to offer up "all the
merits of the heart of Jesus." She promises to help
Bernadette to "thank the holy Virgin right up to the end."
She also adds a few words in a low voice. She did not
recount what those words were, but she did tell us
Bernadette's response: "Ah! I thank you!" (L 589).

It is the last time that the sun will set on Bernadette.

The Last Night

That night (April 15-April 16) she is attended by a novice,
Sister Alphonse Guerre.:

I sat down by her bed to be ready to aid her.

From time to time her suffering wrung a feeble groan from her, and this made me start in my chair. She asked me quite a few times to help her turn over so that she could find a little relief. Her meager body was almost raw, and you could say that she was resting on her sores.

So the two of us tried to get together and work out this difficult maneuver. I took the foot on her bad leg...and I tried to follow the movements of her body so that she could turn over all at once without having to bend the knee. I noticed that during that interminable night not a word of impatience or dissatisfaction escaped her lips...Everything else has slipped my mind (L 590).

In the morning she is visited by Mother Marie-Louise Bourgeot. Bernadette, still alert, remembers to give her a picture for one of her nuns in Beaumont: Sister Madeleine Bounaix. At 11:30 A.M. she asks to be helped up.

We fix her up in the armchair. She notices the time when the clock strikes...and asks pardon of the companions around her who have been made late for their midday meal because of her (L 593).

Final Hours with the Crucifix

Mother Éléonore Cassagnes recounts that she kept looking at the crucifix across from her armchair (L 593). Between noon and 1:00 P.M. she "tries to take a little food but does not succeed" (Mother Joséphine Forestier):

Her state of extreme weakness struck me...
I thought it my duty to inform the
infirmarian and to alert the community
(L 594).

Father Febvre comes in, hears her Confession once
again, and recites the prayers for the dying with her. She
repeats his words "in a feeble but distinct voice" (L 595).
Her gaze is still focused intently on the crucifix hanging
on the opposite wall (L 593 II). The chaplain picks up the
account here:

In a quiet moment I offered her
encouragement with the biblical words
from the Song of Songs (8:8): "Set me as a
seal on your heart."
    We saw her clutch her crucifix and
place it on her heart, squeezing it tightly.
She wanted it to stay right on that spot. I
think someone tied it there to make sure
that it would not be shifted by any
involuntary movement caused by her pain
(L 596).

With this gesture Bernadette apparently sought to
seal her covenant with the crucified Jesus. Between 1:30
P.M. and 2:00 o'clock, Mother Éléonore resumes the
conversation with Bernadette.

"You are on the cross."

Bernadette stretches her two hands towards the
crucifix: "My Jesus! Oh! How much I love you!" (L 597).

At 2:15 P.M. one of her sister nuns resumes the
conversation with her: "My sister, are you suffering a
great deal?"

"All that is good for heaven."

"I am going to ask our Immaculate Mother...to give
you some consolation."

"No," says the patient, "no consolations, only strength
and patience" (L 599; deposition of Father Febvre).

Then Bernadette remembers the blessing that Pius IX had granted her for the hour of her death. She wants to hold the paper in her hands—

> to benefit from its actual application. We
> pointed out to her that this was not
> necessary, that all she had to do was
> invoke the name of Jesus and have the
> proper intention (L 600).

At that moment she tries to raise herself up, putting her right hand on the armchair for support. She looks up to heaven and brings her left hand to her forehead. Her eyes are piercing, and for a few moments they stare at some fixed point. Her features express calmness, serenity and, at the same time, a certain melancholic gravity. Then, in an indescribable tone of voice, suggesting surprise more than pain, and with ever growing expression, she exclaims three times: "Oh! Oh! Oh!" Her whole body trembles (L 601). It is 2:30 P.M.

At 2:55 P.M. the bell rings for the litanies which the community recite daily in the chapel. Bernadette 'wishes to take a little rest." Her confessor and the nuns leave her.

"The holy Virgin will come down to meet you," says someone by way of encouragement.

"Oh yes, I hope so," Bernadette replies.

Around 3:00 P.M. the patient seems to be suffering from some indescribable inner agony. She seizes her crucifix (the one which Bishop de Ladoue brought her from Rome in 1877), contemplates it lovingly for a moment, and then slowly kisses each of Christ's wounds (L 605).

Sister Nathalie, who comes in at that moment, finds her absorbed in contemplating her crucifix:

> Suddenly Bernadette raises her head.. with
> an indescribable look...
> "My dear Sister, pardon me...pray for
> me...*pray for me.*"

> [Sister Nathalie] and the two
> infirmarians fall on their knees to pray. The
> patient joins in their invocations, repeating
> them in a low voice (L 606).
> Then she recollects herself for a few
> moments, her head leaning towards the
> infirmarian on her left. Then, with an
> expression of pain and of total
> abandonment, she raises her eyes to
> heaven, stretches her arms to the cross,
> and gives out with a loud cry: "My God!"
> (L 607)

A shudder runs through the three
nuns still kneeling by her side.

Once again Bernadette joins in the prayers being said
by her companions: "Holy Mary, Mother of God..."

She comes to herself once again and twice repeats
the phrase:

> Holy Mary, Mother of God, pray for me,
> *poor sinner* (L 608).

She looks intently at Sister Nathalie and stretches her
arms out to her. Sister Nathalie, who has worked with the
deaf, does not need words to know what people are
trying to say. Her inquiring look tells Bernadette that she
knows Bernadette wants something of her, though not a
word has been spoken. Bernadette realizes that.

"It's that you would help me," Bernadette says "in a
loud voice" (L 609).

Sister Nathalie recalls the promise she had made to
Bernadette the evening before: to help her "thank the
holy Virgin right up to the end." A few moments later

> the patient signs for something to drink.
> She makes a big Sign of the Cross, lays
> hold of the decanter offered her, takes a
> few sips a couple of times and, lowering
> her head, gently delivers up her soul (L 611).

Sister Gabriel de Vigouroux, the infirmarian, enters the room at the last moment:

> I arrived just on time to be there when she breathed her last, supported on my arm. She was holding her crucifix in her hand, supporting it on her heart. Someone had even attached it, I think. She was turned on her right side, but she closed her eyes. I recall having had trouble closing her right eye, which opened several times (L 611).

Lasserre saw her in death (notes Zola in his 1892 *Journal de Lourdes*). He says "that she was very beautiful."

SAINTE BERNADETTE dans sa Châsse

"Unless a grain of wheat falls on the ground and dies it remains only a single grain; but if it dies, it yields a rich harvest."   Jn 12:24

Armchair in which Bernadette died.

Journal Dedicated to the Queen of Heaven

How happy my soul was, good Mother,
when I had the good fortune to gaze upon you!
How I love to recall the pleasant moments spent
under your gaze, so full of kindness and mercy for us.

Yes, tender Mother, you stooped down to earth
to appear to a mere child...You, the Queen
of heaven and earth, deigned to make use
of the most fragile thing in the world's eyes.

Saint Bernadette, 1866
Journal Dedicated to the Queen of Heaven
(ESB, p. 187)

Key to Abbreviations

This book is addressed to the general public, and so references have been reduced to the minimum. The citations used in this book refer readers to basic works containing substantive basis and proof for what is written here, as well as supplementary details. The following abbreviations identify these sources:

A   File A of Cros Archives, Mainly A III, A VI and A VII: Minutes of the 1878-1880 investigation.

ANDL   *Annales de Notre-Dame de Lourdes.*

Arch   Archives

AZUN   T.M.J. Azun de Bernétas, *La Grotte des Pyrénées,* Tarbes, Larrieu, 1961.

B   R. Laurentin, *Bernadette vous parle,* Paris, Lethielleux, 1972, 2 Volumes. A detailed life.

BARBET   J. Barbet, *Bernadette Soubirous,* Pau, 1909, citations from the Tarbes edition of 1923.

CROS   L.J.M. Cros, *Histoire de N.D. de Lourdes,* Paris, Beauchesne, 1927, 3 Volumes.

D   R. Laurentin, *Lourdes, documents authentiques* (in collaboration with B. Billet), 7 Volumes, Paris, Lethielleux, 1957-1966.

ESB   A. Ravier, *Écrits de Sainte Bernadette,* Paris, Lethielleux, 1961.

FORCADE   Augustin Forcade, Bishop of Nevers (in the time of Bernadette), *Notice sur la vie de Soeur Marie-Bernarde,* Aix, Makaire, 1879.

GUYNOT   E. Guynot, *Sainte Bernadette.* The numbers which follow this name indicate the date of various editions, in which the material chosen is varied.

H   R. Laurentin, *Lourdes, histoire authentique des apparitions,* 6 Volumes, Paris, Lethielleux, 1961-1964. The basis for the apparitions.

L   R. Laurentin and M.T. Bourgeade, *Logia de Bernadette,* 3 Volumes, Paris, Lethielleux, 1971. A critical study of Bernadette's words and sayings from 1866 to 1879. The number which follows the (L) indicates the *number of the saying in question.* The page is indicated afterwards only when there is good reason.

LHA　　　R. Laurentin, *Lourdes. Histoire authentique des apparitions,* 6 volumes, Paris, Lethielleux, 1961-1964.

OG　　　M. Olphe-Galliard, *Lourdes 1858. Témoins de l'événement,* Paris, Lethielleux, 1957.

PANev　　*Procès apostolique de béatification,* Nevers, 1917-1919. 8 volumes; manuscripts of 4,516 pages. Archives of Nevers and secret archives of the Vatican.

PATarb　　*Procès apostolique de béatification,* Tarbes, 1915-1919. Archives of Nevers and secret archives of the Vatican.

PONev　　*Procès de l'Ordinaire pour la béatification* de Bernadette, 1908-1909, 6 volumes; manuscripts of 1,550 folios (3,100 pages). Archives of the Sisters of Nevers and secret archives of the Vatican.

R　　　　R. Laurentin, *Récit authentique des apparitions,* Paris, Lethielleux, 1966. An abridged version of H.

RC　　　*Registre des contemporains, 1907,* Nevers Archives. Register of Bernadette's contemporaries.

RSL　　　*Recherches sur Lourdes,* compiled in Lourdes by B. Billet.

SEMPE　　R. Sempé and Duboé, *Notre-Dame de Lourdes par ses premiers chapelains,* Paris, Letouzey, 9th edition, 316 pages, 1931. (This volume was first published in serial form in the *Annales de Notre-Dame de Lourdes,* from August 1868 to November 1869.)

V　　　　B. Billet, *Bernadette. Une vocation...* 2nd edition, Paris, Lethielleux, 1965.

VEDERE　*Bernadette et Jeanne Vedere,* Auros, 1933. (We cite this text following the two handwritten texts that were lightly edited for the publication cited).

[ ]　　　Indicates additions

Photographs are taken from the collections of R. Laurentin, Von Matt, Durand and Viron.

Author's Appendix

Note on the Lourdes *Patois* and the Term *Aquerò*

This account has not been fictionalized. The names, the events, the dialogues, and the quotes have been drawn scrupulously from authenticated documents. Fictitious elements, which still abound today in many works, have been excluded. The correctness of each detail can be verified in my other volumes, where I have tried to authenticate the account of the apparitions and the life of Bernadette: *Lourdes, documents authentiques* (D); *Lourdes, histoire authentique des apparitions* (H); and *Logia de Bernadette* (L). I use abbreviations to refer to these volumes and others. The full list can be found in the Key to Abbreviations section.

The Dialect of Lourdes

Here I would like to say a brief word about the local dialect or *patois* of Lourdes. As is mentioned in this narrative, Bernadette did not speak standard French. Up to the time of the apparitions, she spoke only "the *patois* of Lourdes," as she called it. It is in this dialect of the *langue d'oc* (or *langue occitane)* group that she received the communications of the Virgin Mary. For the sake of authenticity, this account records a few typical expressions in that dialect that are indispensable to our story.

But how are we to transcribe that dialect? It is a hotly disputed question between two schools of thought: the *École Occitane* and the *Ecole Gaston Fébus.* The orthography of the two schools differs, and neither coincides with the graphemes improvised by the contemporary documents. In another work, *Lourdes, histoire authentique* (H), I explored these issues in some detail and tried to settle them. In that work readers will find that each utterance of the Virgin Mary is examined and that some confirmation is sought between the orthography of the *sources* and the transcriptions based on the principles of the two schools. My present work, however, is addressed to the public at large and so we cannot tackle such problems here. I have chosen to transcribe the *patois* as close to the documents as possible. However, I have adopted two specific conventions to obviate the controversies and feelings of contempt that always abound in matters of local speech, be it in the case of La Salette, Lourdes, or Pontmain:

1.) I use the accent mark *only as a stress accent.* This usage was unknown in Bernadette's day, but it is imperative today. If I were to use grave (`) or acute (´) accents in a more precise way, I would be reproached by specialists whose competence I respect.

2.) Hence the reader should remember that in the *langue d'oc* group of dialects, and particularly in the dialect of Lourdes, there is no mute /e/. It is to be pronounced *at all times,* with an acute or a grave accent as the case may be (é or è). This point is especially important in trying to avoid confusion over the word *Aquerò,* as we shall see in the next section of this Appendix.

I would like to thank Father Point and the members of the Missionaries of the Immaculate Conception, natives of Lourdes, who examined my transcriptions and gave me the benefit of their knowledge.

Aquerò

That is the word which Bernadette used to designate the apparition so long as the latter refused to identify itself: i.e., up until March 25, 1858. The dialect word poses a problem, since it can have two different meanings depending on where the accent goes.

One possibility is *Aquéro.* If the accent is put on the second syllable as here, then we have a two-syllable word because the /o/ of the final syllable is silent. In this case the word is equivalent to *celle-la* in ordinary French: "that one" or "that thing there" (feminine gender). This word is in widespread use in the dialects of the *langue d'oc* group.

The other possibility is *Aquerò.* If the accent is on the final syllable, then the word means: 'that thing' (neuter gender). The form is common in the Lourdes dialect, but rare elsewhere.

How did Bernadette pronounce the word? The documents that I re-examined for the centenary leave no doubt about the matter. *The second alternative is the one understood by all those who talked with Bernadette prior to March 25*: Jacomet, Prosecutor Dutour, the journalist Romain Capdeville, Estrade, his sister Emmanuelite, Sister Augustine, Marie Dufo, and

Pimorin (texts reproduced in LHA 3, pp. 142-144). Pimorin is
especially explicit on this point. On March 21, 1858, four days
before the apparition reveals her name, he writes: "The lady to
whom she (Bernadette) never gives any other designation but
that of *Aquerò—Cela* ('that thing'). There is no disagreement
among the witnesses on this point. No one translates the word
in terms of the first alternative: *celle-la.* Even those who did not
dare to record the term *Aquerò* directly attest to it indirectly by
using some abstract term to translate Bernadette's statements.
Thus the doctors who examined her on March 27 refer to "the
object."

This term used by Bernadette, and kept secret for a long
time by the historians of Lourdes, is somewhat shocking. But it
is not scandalous, as some might think. It expresses
Bernadette's respect for the ineffable. It is completely in accord
with what we call negative theology (*theologia negativa*). The
mystics, whether educated or uneducated, often talk about
God's light in terms of night, and speak of God's transcendent
existence in terms that remind us of nothingness. It all stems
from a deep concern not to use common, ordinary, inadequate
language to describe what is "wholly other."

Those who have a low opinion of the common people and
their intelligence sometimes claim that a simple creature like
Bernadette could not have gone so far in her use of language.
The truth is, of course, that the common people have an
understanding of God which is not that of the wise and
educated of this world. The gospel message tells us that.

Bernadette in death.